Treasures of the Taylorian

Series One: Reformation Pamphlets

Volume 2

Martin Luther

Sermon von Ablass und Gnade
Sermon on Indulgences and Grace

95 Theses

Edited by Howard Jones,
Martin Keßler, Henrike Lähnemann,
and Christina Ostermann

Series editor: Henrike Lähnemann

Taylor Institution Library, Oxford, 2018

First published in March 2018 by Taylor Institution Library.
Reprinted with corrections April 2018

http://www.bodleian.ox.ac.uk/taylor

A number of digital downloads to accompany this edition are available from *editions.mml.ox.ac.uk*. They include:

- A podcast of the *Sermon von Ablass und Gnade*
- A fold-your-own pamphlet facsimile of both copies
- A pdf ebook of the text
- An open access version of this booklet

The facsimiles are of the two Taylor Institution Library copies of Martin Luther's *Sermon von Ablass und Gnade*
- Arch. 8° G. 1518 (5), Basel: Pamphilus Gengenbach 1518
- Arch. 8° G. 1518 (6), Leipzig: Valentin Schumann 1518.

The cover image is from the title-page of Arch. 8° G. 1518 (6).

Typesetting, digital edition and cover design by Emma Huber, Subject Consultant for German, Taylor Institution Library

ISBN 978-0-9954564-2-6

Taylor Institution Library, St Giles, Oxford, OX1 3NA

Table of Contents

The floral border is from the title page of Arch. 8° G. 1518 (5).

Preface: The Taylorian Resources

Emma Huber

The *Sermon von Ablass und Gnade* (*Sermon on Indulgences and Grace*) is the second in the Taylor Institution Library's series of Reformation Pamphlets. Thanks are due to John Flood, Alexander Huber, Christiane Rehagen, Edmund Wareham, and those who offered feedback on the first volume in the series (*Ein Sendbrief vom Dolmetschen*), and on the draft of the second.

Additional material has hitherto been provided on blogs.bodleian.ox.ac.uk/taylor-reformation. With the launch of the second pamphlet, we are migrating this content to a more permanent home, the new Taylor Editions website (editions.mml.ox.ac.uk), which also offers a new way of exploring the library's holdings. The texts in this resource are created by members of the Faculty of Medieval and Modern Languages during an eight-week Digital Editions course run by library staff. The images and TEI-encoded transcriptions are created by course participants using equipment available to all readers in the library. The editions are available to use and reuse.

The Reformation Series is therefore now available in multiple formats for use in a wide range of settings. The print texts are also available as open access pdf ebooks. All the material from the books, including the introductory material, images, transcriptions, and translations, with the added benefit of hyperlinks and the possibility of zooming in to colour images, is now also available via the website, along with supplementary resources, such as a fold-your-own pamphlet and podcasts of the texts being read aloud.

Additional pamphlets, not yet available in print form, can be viewed online, and we also welcome contributions of transcriptions and translations of all or part of a pamphlet. We hope that this may give an added dimension to translation and history of the book classes.

Ill. 1: Woodcut showing the selling of indulgences
Heinrich Vogtherr the Elder (20 x 15), Taylor Institution Library, Arch. 8°G. 1519 (8/8) *On Aplas von Rom kan man wol selig werden,* [Augsburg: Melchior Ramminger 1521] VD16 O 527

Introduction

The *Sermon von Ablass und Gnade* (*Sermon on Indulgences and Grace*) is a seminal text for the Reformation: it is the first vernacular statement of Luther's views on the question which led to his break with Rome; the first printed work of his to reach a mass audience; and the first example of the direct, arresting style which became the hallmark of his German writings. The work hit the market 500 years ago, in the second half of March 1518, five months after the posting of the *95 Theses*, and within three years at least 24 editions had been printed in various parts of Germany and Switzerland. Our volume is based on two of these editions, copies of which are held in the Taylor Institution Library, and presents a guide to the theological, historical, material, linguistic, and stylistic importance of this work.

The *Sermon* rejects scholastic teaching about indulgences and proposes instead a theology of grace. Luther meant the *Sermon* as an accessible summary of his views, and for the modern reader it is still the most succinct account of Luther's side in the indulgence controversy, serving as an introduction to the more technical *95 Theses* which are also included in Latin and English in this edition. The theological and historical context of the *Sermon* and *95 Theses* is complex and dates back centuries before the actual texts. We explain this background and provide an evaluation of both works in 'Theological and Historical Background'.

This volume includes facsimiles of the two Taylorian copies on facing pages along with an edition based on the Leipzig edition and a new translation into modern English. We offer a detailed guide to the book history in 'The Taylorian Copies' (including an analysis of the woodcuts in the Basel edition and the marginalia added to the Taylorian copy of the Leipzig edition), a preview to the follow-up pamphlets in the debate (cf. ill. 2), and an account of the acquisition history.

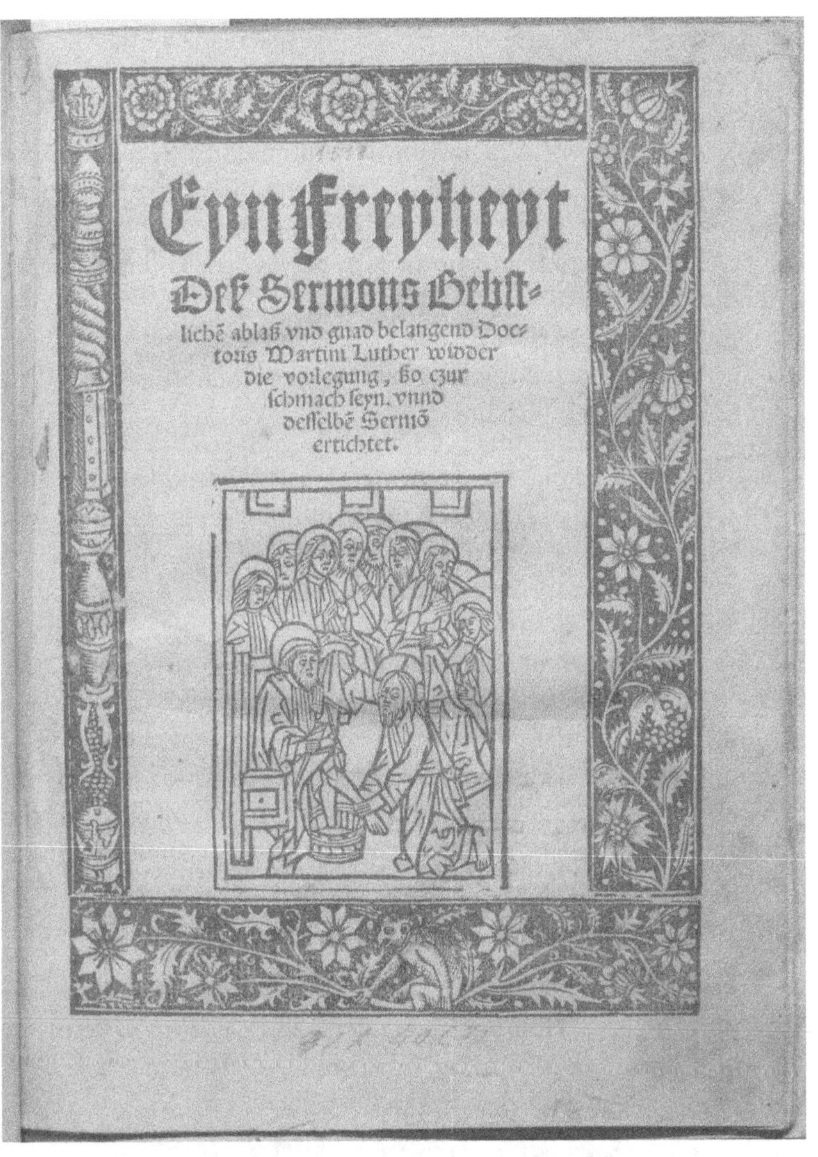

Eyn Freyheyt
Deß Sermons Bebst-
lichē ablaß vnd gnad belangend Doc-
toris Martini Luther widder
die vorlegung, ßo czur
schmach seyn. vnnd
desselbē Sermō
ertichtet.

Ill. 2: Luther's follow-up pamphlet in the Taylorian Collection
Eyn Freyheyt Deß Sermons Bebstlichē ablaß vnd gnad belangend,
Taylor Institution Library, Arch. 8° G. 1523 (43/2)
[Leipzig: Valentin Schumann 1518], VD16 L 4741

By putting his arguments in the vernacular, Luther could simultaneously address experts and win over the general public, whereas only the former was possible in Latin. This first publishing success was followed by a stream of sermons, treatises, and other pastoral, polemical, and political writings over the next few years, all written in an evolving but distinctive style of German. In 'Language and Style', we offer a linguistic analysis of the *Sermon*, highlighting differences from modern German, dialect features of these two editions (East Central German and Low Alemannic), and some of the stylistic qualities which were to characterize Luther's German writing for the rest of his career.

This is the first time that these two editions have been made available to a modern audience. To make the Early New High German text in its original spelling accessible for students of Linguistics as well as Theology and History, a guide on 'How to Read the *Sermon*' is included. Of the two Taylorian copies, the one published in Leipzig by Valentin Schumann is probably more similar to what Luther wrote than the Basel one by Pamphilus Gengenbach, since the text is closer to the earliest Wittenberg version of the *Sermon*. We therefore use the Leipzig edition as the basis for the facing transcription to the new translation. At editions.mml.ox.ac.uk the Basel edition has also been transcribed as a further example of printed material and of the variation that could exist between different versions of the same work – in appearance, dialect, and content.

Emma Huber, Howard Jones, Martin Keßler,
Henrike Lähnemann, and Christina Ostermann
Oxford, March 2018

Getruckt nach Christ geburt Tausent
fünffhundert vnd ym achtzehēdē Jar.

Anno Domini 1518. End of the Leipzig print of the *Sermon*
Taylor Institution Library, Arch. 8° G. 1518 (6), A4r

1. Theological and Historical Background

Martin Keßler

Luther's *95 Theses* are widely considered to mark the beginning of the Reformation. Over the course of four centuries, beginning in Saxony in 1617, 31 October has established itself as the pivotal date in Reformation memory.[1] While the epoch-making, heroic image of Luther nailing his series of disputation theses to the doors of Wittenberg's Castle Church has been questioned and debated for six decades, it is clear that such as an act would have been anything but spectacular.[2] Disputation theses were addressed to the academic public, accordingly written in Latin, displayed on the local church doors which served as the university's notice board, and sometimes also sent to other scholars. If this is what Luther did, he did not stop there, for he also sent his theses to senior representatives of the local church hierarchy. On 31 October 1517, the eve of All Saints' Day, he attached his theses to a letter to Archbishop Albrecht of Mainz and Magdeburg.[3] In his own account from 1518 and in later years, Luther

---

[1] Thomas Kaufmann, Das Reformationsjubiläum 1617, in: Thomas Kaufmann, Dreißigjähriger Krieg und Westfälischer Friede. Kirchengeschichtliche Studien zur lutherischen Konfessionskultur, Tübingen 1998 (Beiträge zur historischen Theologie 104), 10–23.

[2] The best summary of the earlier discussions is in a series of articles in: Geschichte in Wissenschaft und Unterricht. Zeitschrift des Verbandes der Geschichtslehrer Deutschlands 16/11 (1965), 661–99. For more recent considerations see Joachim Ott and Martin Treu (eds), Luthers Thesenanschlag – Faktum oder Fiktion, Leipzig 2008 (Schriften der Stiftung Luthergedenkstätten in Sachsen-Anhalt 9) and Uwe Wolff (ed.), Iserloh. Der Thesenanschlag fand nicht statt, Basel 2013 (Studia oecumenica Friburgensia 61).

[3] Luther's writings (WA) and letters (WA.Br) are quoted from D. Martin Luthers Werke. Kritische Gesamtausgabe, 120 vols, Weimar 1883–2009;

mentions also having written to Hieronymus Scultetus, Bishop of Brandenburg and Havelberg.[4] If these recollections are accurate, Luther was engaging with two senior echelons of the church right from the start. As it turned out, these formal steps, together with the theological content of what he wrote and the legal claims he made about the sale in indulgences at the time, triggered a chain of events that led within three years to Luther's excommunication.

What made the *95 Theses* special and how can one best study this classic piece of Reformation history? The present edition provides various answers and offers one practical suggestion: ease yourself in gently by reading the *Sermon on Indulgences and Grace* and then proceed to the theses. Why? Because – to put it bluntly – the *95 Theses* would otherwise be largely incomprehensible. Even scholarly readers accept that the theses taken on their own demand explanation and exposition, but this simply illustrates the nature of disputation theses.[5] They were intended for an academic debate in which authorities and arguments were tossed back and forth. In academic disputations the pros and cons were represented by two sides – individuals or groups –, those of opponent and respondent. The opponent's task was to cite counter-arguments to the theses – whether from biblical authority, patristic sources, theological doctrine, legal tradition, or general reason and experience –, while the respondent had to evaluate and develop the arguments. Luther's *95 Theses* fit into this pattern: they provide the basis for a more detailed and structured exchange, and they are neither sufficient nor

---

here: WA.Br 1, 110–12. Parts of the letter are translated by Hans J. Hillerbrand (ed.), The Protestant Reformation. Revised edition, New York [etc.] 2009, 25–27.

[4] Cf. WA.Br 1, 113–14, and for further important references Hans Volz, Martin Luthers Thesenanschlag und dessen Vorgeschichte, Weimar 1959, 19–23.

[5] Cf. Anselm Schubert, Libertas Disputandi. Luther und die Leipziger Disputation als akademisches Streitgespräch, in: Zeitschrift für Theologie und Kirche 105 (2008), 411–42.

self-explanatory. They invite contradiction or agreement on the basis of solid authority. The author's own comments, clarifications, or conclusions were sometimes documented in subsequent explanations. When dealing with a series of academic theses like Luther's, one thus has to study both the theses themselves and (if available) the *resolutiones* or *propositiones* which followed. In Luther's case, we have the *resolutiones* to most of his early disputation theses, including these. If one hopes to get the gist of the early Reformation by reading the *95 Theses*, one must also digest Luther's explanations – and indeed be aware of their sheer size: the two oldest surviving editions of the theses themselves are broadsides;[6] the corresponding *Resolutiones disputationum de indulgentiarum virtute* come to 120 pages in the smaller quarto format.[7]

Despite their length, Luther must have handwritten – or had written – at least three manuscript copies of his *Resolutiones*. One version became the basis for the eventual print that was completed by August 1518. The other two reveal whom Luther intended to keep informed about the exchange of arguments: the first of these manuscripts was sent in February 1518 to Hieronymus Scultetus to satisfy the requirements of episcopal supervision and the second, three months later, to the Pope via Johann von Staupitz.[8] Luther's letter to Scultetus survives and offers an interesting summary of previous events; it is the earliest comprehensive account by Luther himself of what happened. According to this document, 'new and unheard-of

---

[6] Josef Benzing and Helmut Claus, Lutherbibliographie. Verzeichnis der gedruckten Schriften Martin Luthers bis zu dessen Tod, 1, Baden-Baden [2]1989 (Bibliotheca bibliographica Aureliana 10), 16, nos 87–88. The two known broadsides are from Nuremberg and Leipzig. It is an on-going debate whether there was an initial print from Wittenberg which was lost. It has been recently suggested that Luther was involved in the production of the Leipzig print; see Thomas Kaufmann, Druckerpresse statt Hammer, in: Frankfurter Allgemeine Zeitung, 31 Oct. 2016, 6.

[7] Cf. WA 1, 523.

[8] WA.Br 1, 138–40, 525–27.

doctrines' regarding apostolic indulgences had started to spread from the latest sales that had reached the region.[9] One has to bear in mind when reading these words that 'new' teaching was synonymous with heresy. The nature of apostolic doctrines is that they are old and go back to the origins of Christianity. Accordingly, this is Luther pointing out heretical elements in current church practices. Luther explains that his own involvement springs from a sense of spiritual and theological responsibility: simple and educated people alike have approached him for his own professional assessment. Luther claims to have initially responded in a reserved, non-committal way, but that this had backfired, since it increased and sharpened the criticism he faced. His solution was not to take sides, but to open up a debate, 'until the holy church' had taken a binding decision on the topic.[10] Hence 'I sent out the disputation, inviting and asking everyone publicly, and asking the most learned scholars I knew privately, so that they might at least reveal their opinion in writing'.[11] The reactions disappointed Luther. Scholars did not answer: on the contrary, the text was circulated more widely and was mistaken for 'assertions' instead of theses intended for a debate.[12] If one turns to the original invitation to the *95 Theses* at the beginning of the translated text in this edition, it corresponds with the summary just given. It has to be stressed, however, how unusual this procedure was. Luther's introduction does not fix a date for the disputation and it does not state who the protagonists would be. In Wittenberg there is only one other example of such an arrangement for a disputation. Six months earlier, in April 1517, Luther's theological colleague Andreas Bodenstein, named after his Franconian native town of Karlstadt, issued a series of 152 theses which documented his farewell to the scholastic teaching traditions in which he had himself excelled as Wittenberg's most prolific and versatile exponent, and showcased

---

[9] WA.Br 1, 138.

[10] WA.Br 1, 139.

[11] WA.Br 1, 139 (reading *novi* instead of the conjecture *nosti*).

[12] WA.Br 1, 139.

his new affiliation with an Augustinian-based theology of grace.[13] Karlstadt, too, had left the intended time and participants open. His correspondence reveals that he had hoped to attract the leading scholars in the territory to take part in a major disputation in Wittenberg.[14] It has been suggested that Karlstadt might have been inspired in this format by Pico della Mirandola who had planned to debate 900 theses before a huge audience in 1487.[15] Neither Karlstadt's nor Luther's theses led to an actual disputation. Still, in Luther's case it is clear that the intended audience would have been a locally or regionally restricted academic one.[16] In March 1518 Luther confirmed this to his former Wittenberg colleague from the Faculty of Law, Christoph Scheurl, who had returned to his hometown Nuremberg to take up a senior municipal post.[17]

To some extent, Scheurl was responsible for the theses being more widely publicized and distributed, especially in the south of Germany. One of the two known broadsides, printed like a poster just on one side of folio-sized paper, is from Nuremberg and was forwarded by Scheurl to Johannes Eck, a rising theological star at the University of Ingolstadt. Scheurl has been described as an 'enthusiast of friendship'[18] or the 'platform and networking service of German

---

[13] Edited by Ulrich Bubenheimer and Martin Keßler, in: Thomas Kaufmann (ed.), Kritische Gesamtausgabe der Schriften und Briefe Andreas Bodensteins von Karlstadt, 1/1: 1507–1517, Gütersloh 2017 (Quellen und Forschungen zur Reformationsgeschichte 90/1), 499–511.

[14] Ulrich Bubenheimer and Martin Keßler, Einleitung, in: Kaufmann, Gesamtausgabe, 485–98, here: 494–95.

[15] For the discovery and documentation of Karlstadt's knowledge of the text, see the introduction and edition by Ulrich Bubenheimer, in: Kaufmann, Gesamtausgabe, 365–71.

[16] Cf. WA.Br 1, 113–14.

[17] WA.Br 1, 152.

[18] Gustav Bauch, Christoph Scheurl in Wittenberg, in: Neue Mitteilungen aus dem Gebiete historisch-antiquarischer Forschungen 21 (1903), 33–42, here: 33.

humanism'[19]. His goal was to instigate and encourage relationships between his own numerous friends. Attempts to recommend Eck and Luther to one another started off promisingly, but did not really develop. Scheurl had sent disputation theses from Eck to Wittenberg in April 1517; Luther did not reply directly, but asked Scheurl to forward his so-called *Disputatio contra scholasticam theologiam* to Eck in October 1517.[20] By the end of the first week of 1518, Scheurl had distributed the *95 Theses* widely. He had sent them to Augsburg and Ingolstadt; one of his friends had produced a German translation; and Eck had been responsive enough to announce that he would walk ten miles in order to debate with Luther.[21] Interestingly, what Eck did with the *95 Theses* was no different from what Luther had done: he presented them to his local bishop and offered an annotated version.[22] Eck's remarks show that he, too, saw potential heresy, but this time on Luther's side. On eleven consecutive theses he remarked that they were 'crude and tasteless, or rather they taste like

[19] Johann Peter Wurm, Johannes Eck und die Disputation von Leipzig 1519. Vorgeschichte und unmittelbare Folgen, in: Markus Hein and Armin Kohnle (eds), Die Leipziger Disputation 1519. 1. Leipziger Arbeitsgespräch zur Reformation, Leipzig 2011 (Herbergen der Christenheit, special vol. 18), 95–106, here: 96.

[20] Peter Fabisch and Erwin Iserloh (eds), Dokumente zur Causa Lutheri (1517–1521), 1: Das Gutachten des Prierias und weitere Schriften gegen Luthers Ablaßthesen (1517–1518), Münster 1988 (Corpus Catholicorum 41), 376–77.

[21] Fabisch/Iserloh, Dokumente, 377. For the political background to the German translation see Wilhelm Ernst Winterhager, Die Verkündigung des St. Petersablasses in Mittel und Nordeuropa 1515–1519, in: Andreas Rehberg (ed.), Ablasskampagnen des Spätmittelalters. Luthers Thesen von 1517 im Kontext, Berlin 2017 (Bibliothek des Deutschen Historischen Instituts in Rom 132), 565–610, here: 594.

[22] Fabisch/Iserloh, Dokumente, 378–79. Winterhager, Verkündigung, 595–96, reconstructs the personal and structural involvement of the bishop of Eichstätt in questioning the indulgence campaign.

Bohemia'.[23] The 'Bohemian poison',[24] as he also calls it, was a reference to the last great heresy that had brought war to an entire nation: that of Jan Hus, the scholar from Prague who had taken up the theological promptings of the Oxford theologian John Wyclif.[25] Eck went on to become Luther's and Karlstadt's opponent in the Leipzig Debate in 1519, the Reformation's first actual disputation that reached a wide audience.[26] Following the Leipzig Debate, Eck travelled to Rome and worked out the papal bull that threatened Luther with excommunication in 1520.

So far we have looked at the nature of academic disputations and found that, to some extent, Luther kept to the established procedure, but also opened it up. What might strike one as puzzling in all this is Luther's incidental and yet central claim: that the church's teaching on indulgence had not been finalized. Was this the case, and what are indulgences anyway? Luther's first thesis introduces the term by referring to Matthew 4: 17 and Jesus's call to 'Do penance' (or 'Repent'), 'for the kingdom of heaven has come near.' He could just as well have quoted Matthew 3: 2, since Jesus himself is taking up the words of John the Baptist. Penance or penitence (lat. *poenitentia*)[27] initially described the one and only life-changing turning point in an individual's development towards God. The Greek 'metanoia' (μετάνοια) can refer to this very process: a complete and utter change to a human's inner disposition or direction. Penance and baptism almost coincided as the key moment of rearranging the relationship to God. Implicitly this involved the hope of living without deviating

---

[23] Fabisch/Iserloh, Dokumente, 435.

[24] Fabisch/Iserloh, Dokumente, 431.

[25] On the various aspects of this topic see František Šmahel (ed.), A companion to Jan Hus, Leiden [etc.] 2015 (Brill's companions to the Christian tradition, 54). Specifically on Hus and indulgences, see Pavel Soukup, Jan Hus und der Prager Ablassstreit von 1412, in: Rehberg, Ablasskampagnen, 523–64, here: 485–500.

[26] Hein/Kohnle, Disputation.

[27] See the note to thesis 1 of Luther's *95 Theses* in this edition, p. 33.

further from God. But this raised a fresh problem: What happened if followers relapsed? From this question a shift in terminology transformed the fundamental dimension of distance from God into a selection of outrageous acts. In particular, three main sins developed from the Ten Commandments: denying or renouncing God ('apostasy'), adultery, and murder. Various options were considered about how to handle these and other violations. A radical view was expressed in Hebrews 6: 4–8: Whoever sins after baptism is to be excluded from the church for good. It is questionable whether this position was ever actually applied. Another position was taken in a visionary text, the *Shepherd of Hermas*, written around 100 A.D. After baptism, so the suggestion goes, the sinner could be reintegrated into the congregation, but only once, 'since for the servants of God there is just *one* penance'.[28] Although Hermas dealt with adultery, it was the offence of apostasy that became a mass phenomenon during the centuries to come. In the wake of various conflicts and schisms, practical solutions evolved.[29] These included bishop Basilius of Caesarea recording a number of authoritative *canones* and suggesting a two-step procedure: public confession by the sinner before the congregation, followed by the church's proposal of special works of penance. Three acts were recommended and performed in particular: prayer, fasting, and almsgiving.[30]

---

[28] Die Apostolischen Väter. Griechisch-deutsche Parallelausgabe auf der Grundlage der Ausgaben von Franz Xaver Funk, Karl Bihlmeyer und Molly Whittaker mit Übersetzungen von M. Dibelius und D.-A. Koch neu übersetzt und herausgegeben von Andreas Lindemann und Henning Paulsen, Tübingen 1992, 380–81 (mandatum IV, 8).

[29] Cf. Wolfram Kinzig and Martin Wallraff, Das Christentum des 3. Jahrhunderts zwischen Anspruch und Wirklichkeit, in: Dieter Zeller (ed.), Christentum I. Von den Anfängen bis zur Konstantinischen Wende, Stuttgart 2002 (Religionen der Menschheit 28), 331–88.

[30] On the biblical background, see the note to §3 of the *Sermon on Indulgences and Grace* in this edition, p. 7.

The transitional period between Late Antiquity and the early Middle Ages witnessed two tendencies.[31] Under one of these tendencies, Augustine highlighted the universal dimensions of sin, with the result that the more extensively sin was understood to refer to all sorts of human attitudes and actions, the more inclusively penance had to be defined. Accordingly, under the second of these tendencies, the act of penance turned into a highly specialised institution during the Middle Ages. Owing to the huge quantity and wide variety of possible offences, the previously public confession turned into a private procedure between culprit and confessor. Highly influential in the British Isles and on the continent were the monks from Ireland and Scotland who drew up detailed, comprehensive catalogues about the appropriate relationship between deeds and penalties.[32] The increase in the number of penalties imposed gave rise to two trends. Firstly, more physically demanding, intensive forms of prayer and fasting started to develop, replacing the more time-consuming activities carried out previously.[33] From this the second trend evolved, which was that not only the act of penance, but also the performer of the act, could be substituted; thus, instead of praying, one could consider giving alms to a monk to do so.[34] The concept of personal commutation[35] was connected with endowments. By funding or supporting monasteries, landlords could expect to profit personally from the monks' prayers. From these, a hierarchy of works developed: collective efforts were better than individual works; the merits of saints surpassed those of the living; and the benefits of Christ trumped all of these as well as the merits of the Apostles.[36] The

[31] Cf. Arnold Angenendt, Grundformen der Frömmigkeit im Mittelalter, München ²2004 (Enzyklopädie deutscher Geschichte 68), 43.

[32] Arnold Angenendt, Das Frühmittelalter. Die abendländische Christenheit von 400 bis 900, Stuttgart [etc.] ²1995, 210.

[33] Angenendt, Frühmittelalter, 211. Arnold Angenendt, Geschichte der Religiosität im Mittelalter, Darmstadt 1997, 637.

[34] Angenendt, Religiosität, 639.

[35] Angenendt, Frühmittelalter, 211. Angenendt, Religiosität, 636–39.

[36] Angenendt, Religiosität, 653–54.

theory of *thesaurus ecclesiae*, the Treasury of Merits that transcended time and space, followed from this and was elaborated academically in the 13th century.[37] Around this time, the term *indulgentia* began to replace older concepts of personal exchange and participation in remission.[38] A related question that had troubled Christians since their early history was God's final judgement: When was this due – after an individual's death or at the end of time? Various concepts developed and even merged.[39] For some, such as saints, John 5: 24–29 might apply and offer direct passage to eternal life. Most, however, had to await a final judgement as described in Matthew 25: 31–46, either individually ('particular judgement') or collectively ('universal judgement'). The potential punishments took time; thus, some souls had to pass through a purifying period before being granted eternal life in heaven. This idea of an intermediate stage has a long tradition[40] and was identified with a purgatory (lat. *purgatorium*) which was more closely defined, theologically and dogmatically, from the 13th century onwards. In precise terms, purgatory offered satisfaction to sinners who had taken the first steps towards penance but who had not managed to perform the acts

---

[37] Gustav Adolf Benrath, Ablaß, in: Gerhard Krause and Müller Müller (eds), Theologische Realenzyklopädie 1, Berlin [etc.] 1977, 347–64, here: 349.

[38] Benrath, Ablaß, 347.

[39] Instructive on the topic is Peter Jezler, Himmel, Hölle, Fegefeuer. Das Jenseits im Mittelalter. Eine Ausstellung des Schweizerischen Landesmuseum in Zusammenarbeit mit dem Schnütgen-Museum und der Mittelalterabteilung des Wallraf-Richartz-Museums der Stadt Köln, München [2]1994.

[40] The classic work is Jacques le Goff, The Birth of Purgatory, London 1984. A solid summary is given by Angenendt, Religiosität, 706–08. For illustrative references, including Bede, see Meinolf Schumacher, Sündenschmutz und Herzensreinheit. Studien zur Metaphorik der Sünde in lateinischer und deutscher Literatur des Mittelalters, München 1996 (Münstersche Mittelalter-Schriften 73), 469.

imposed during their lifetime.[41] This is where indulgence, and indulgences, come in. In 1300, Boniface VIII was the first pope to announce a 'holy year' in which complete remission of sins was offered to visitors to Roman churches who had truly repented and confessed.[42] Acts of penance were accordingly still required and not completely eliminated. Four decades later, Pope Clemens VI's bull *Unigenitus Dei filius* linked the Church's administration of its treasury, the *thesaurus ecclesiae* mentioned above, to the granting of indulgence (i.e. dispensation) for the remission of acts of penance according to specific temporal, local, and personal conditions.[43] The 'holy year' of 1300 illustrates the basic pattern of such conditions and became a model for further holy years, events, and places that involved activities leading to the benefit of indulgence. Starting in Rome, such offers were at first geographically restricted and then became available all over Europe, taking a wide variety of cultural forms. The requirement to be physically present in Rome to be granted indulgence was relaxed and other means of involving relevant places or people were developed. Thus, 'ad instar' indulgences offered measures of indulgence equivalent to what had been defined elsewhere. Connections between, for example, an Italian church (and its offers of indulgence) and venues in Germany were legally fixed – and, as it turned out, later revoked – in papal

---

[41] See the note to thesis 15 of Luther's *95 Theses* in this edition, p. 36. For Martin V's bull *Inter cunctas* from 1418 implying this, see Heinrich Denzinger, Kompendium der Glaubensbekenntnisse und kirchlichen Lehrentscheidungen. Verbessert, erweitert, ins Deutsche übertragen und unter Mitarbeit von Helmut Hoping ed. by Peter Hünermann, Freiburg [etc.] [43]2010, 416, no. 1266. For guidance on further documents relevant to this topic see Denzinger/Hünermann, Kompendium 1692, K10b.

[42] Denzinger/Hünermann, Kompendium, 358, no. 868.

[43] Corpus iuris canonici. Editio Lipsiensis secunda post Aemilii Ludovici Richteri, curas ad librorum manu scriptorum et editionis Romanae fidem recognovit et adnotatione critica instruxit Aemilius Friedberg, 2: Decretalium collectione, Leipzig 1879 [reprint Graz 1959], 1304–06. Denzinger/Hünermann, Kompendium, 384, no. 1025–27.

documents. Relics were another means of participating in the *thesaurus ecclesiae*, and thus, in indulgence, in that they granted personal or physical contact to valued figures of the Christian past.[44] Pilgrimages provided another pathway to indulgence, if they involved visiting places with valued relics on special dates for particular benefits. By the end of the 15th century, indulgences had turned from an exclusive to an extensive good. As in 1300 in Rome, it started off as a locally and temporally restricted offering, and within a century had met with huge demand resulting occasionally in inflationary supply. The national and international dimensions of this have recently been carefully documented and critically reviewed, both for England and the rest of Europe.[45]

Classic Protestant perspectives have tended significantly to devalue and degrade the medieval indulgence trade. Nevertheless, even in older scholarship there is a tradition of reassessing the status of this practice. To some extent one could interpret the magnum opus of Nikolaus Paulus, one of Max Weber's earliest readers, as a counterpart to Weber's own classic study on *The Protestant Ethic and the Spirit of Capitalism*. Paulus's *Geschichte des Ablasses am Ausgang des Mittelalters* sets about interpreting 'indulgences as a social factor in the Middle Ages', as an English translation of one of its central passages

---

[44] Hartmut Kühne, Ostensio reliquiarum. Untersuchungen über Entstehung, Ausbreitung, Gestalt und Funktion der Heiltumsanweisungen im römisch-deutschen Regnum, Berlin 2000 (Arbeiten zur Kirchengeschichte 75). For a brief account with valuable updates: Hartmut Kühne, Ablassvermittlung und Ablassmedien um 1500. Beobachtungen zu Texten, Bildern und Ritualen um 1500 in Mitteldeutschland, in: Rehberg, Ablasskampagnen, 427–57.

[45] R.N. Swanson (ed.), Promissory Notes on the Treasury of Merits. Indulgences in Late Medieval Europe, Leiden 2006 (Brill's Companions to the Christian Tradition 5). R.N. Swanson, Indulgences in Late Medieval England. Passport to paradise?, Cambridge [etc.] 2007. Abigail Firey (ed.), A New History of Penance, Leiden [etc.] 2008 (Brill's Companions to the Christian Tradition 14).

puts it.[46] Indulgence campaigns, according to Paulus, did not just accumulate and alienate capital by exporting it from the territories, but the resources raised were substantially reinvested in local and regional infrastructure, e.g. by promoting and financing the building of new roads that were necessary to access places of worship and pilgrimage. In more recent Protestant scholarship, a new awareness has developed about the spiritual dimensions of indulgence practices. Bernd Moeller thought that he detected a 'trace of the Gospel' in them,[47] before Berndt Hamm noted 'amazing congruences' between the quest for certainty in salvation during the Middle Ages and in the Reformation. According to Hamm, conflicting contemporary responses were close yet different: the acquisition of indulgence involved a 'minimum' of a person's own efforts – receiving the gift of the Gospel none. Hamm calls this move from gradual human involvement to an exclusively divine act a 'quantum leap'.[48] Social and economic studies of German indulgence campaigns are very valuable. Wilhelm Ernst Winterhager[49] challenged the established assumption that the indulgences which were offered enjoyed widespread demand. By comparing the geographical and financial aspects of indulgence sales in the Holy Roman Empire of the German

---

[46] Indulgences as a Social Factor in the Middle Ages. By Nikolaus Paulus. Translated by J. Elliot Ross. With a foreword by Eugene C. Barker, New York 1922. The latest edition of the original work has appeared with some bibliographical additions: Nikolaus Paulus, Geschichte des Ablasses am Ausgang des Mittelalters, 3 vols, Darmstadt [2]2000.

[47] Bernd Moeller, Die letzten Ablaßkampagnen. Luthers Widerspruch gegen den Ablaß in seinem geschichtlichen Zusammenhang, in: Bernd Moeller, Die Reformation und das Mittelalter, Kirchenhistorische Aufsätze, ed. by Johannes Schilling, Göttingen 1991, 53–72, here: 54.

[48] Berndt Hamm, Ablass und Reformation. Erstaunliche Kongruenzen, Tübingen 2016, 159, 168, 244.

[49] Wilhelm Ernst Winterhager, Ablaßkritik als Indikator historischen Wandels vor 1517: Ein Beitrag zu Voraussetzungen und Einordnungen der Reformation, in: Archiv für Reformationsgeschichte 90 (1999), 6–71.

Nation around 1500, he noted two significant developments.[50] In the years before Luther issued the *95 Theses*, organized indulgence sales had narrowed from Empire-wide to territorial campaigns. In big cities such as Nuremberg and Frankfurt am Main, revenues raised by indulgence commissioners fell dramatically in some areas and remained substantial in others. This gave rise to the second development: the territorial campaigns from 1513 onwards shifted their focus from cities to remoter and more rural areas. The infamous campaign organized by Albrecht of Mainz falls into this category.[51] The sale to fund the building of St Peter's Basilica in Rome initially ran from 1515 to 1518 under the direction of the papal legate Arcimboldi in the church provinces of Cologne, Trier, and Bremen and the dioceses of Meißen and Kammin.[52] When Albrecht of Mainz negotiated in 1514 the option of becoming archbishop of Magdeburg, his representatives had strong reservations after the papal side suggested that Albrecht should promote the indulgence campaign as a means of financing the deal.[53] Albrecht's associates had been fully aware of the 'aversion' that this type of campaign was liable to provoke.[54] Others, including Albrecht of Brandenburg-Ansbach, turned down such offers, raising similar concerns.[55] The indulgence trade organized by Albrecht from 1516 to 1518 was confined to his territories of Mainz, Magdeburg, and Brandenburg.[56]

All this has to be borne in mind when we come back to the letter which Luther wrote to Albrecht of Mainz enclosing the *95 Theses*. It refers to practices in neighbouring regions in which a limited, but

---

[50] Winterhager, Ablaßkritik, 22–34.

[51] Winterhager, Verkündigung, 585–86.

[52] For a summary see Winterhager, Ablaßkritik, 23, in more detail Winterhager, Verkündigung, 569–73.

[53] Winterhager, Ablaßkritik, 40. See also Winterhager, Verkündigung, 566–67.

[54] Winterhager, Ablaßkritik, 40.

[55] Winterhager, Ablaßkritik, 40–41; Winterhager, Verkündigung, 575–76.

[56] Winterhager, Ablaßkritik, 23.

highly effective, campaign was being conducted. These areas added up to more than half of the German territories within the Holy Roman Empire. Most of the other parts were handled by Arcimboldi, who was also involved in Sweden and Finland.[57] After Emperor Maximilian had legalized the sale of indulgences in the Holy Roman Empire in 1515,[58] many German territories and cities remained sceptical about the new campaign.[59] Territorial, regional, or local resistance was feasible, but it was subject to Roman and canon law as well as to the pragmatic consideration of how far Albrecht of Mainz was prepared to go in his legal response given the risk of further opposition from other territorial rulers.[60] The Albertine Duke of Saxony, George, actively prevented the sale in his territory, since he objected to the loss of revenue that would have resulted in his area.[61] Like all other sovereigns – except Albrecht of Mainz, the Emperor who had received a substantial sum for his permission,[62] and the Pope – he did not profit from the proceeds. In March 1517, Luther's sovereign, the Elector Frederick the Wise, and his brother Johann responded similarly in their territories,[63] although no documents have been identified to support the notion that they had financial

---

[57] Winterhager, Verkündigung, 567. Maps of the campaign offer an excellent overview of the territories and countries involved: Hartmut Kühne, Enno Bünz, and Peter Wiegand (eds), Johann Tetzel und der Ablass. Begleitband zur Ausstellung 'Tetzel – Ablass – Fegefeuer' in Mönchenkloster und Nikolaikirche Jüterbog vom 8. September bis 26. November 2017, Berlin 2017, 293–98.

[58] Winterhager, Verkündigung, 568.

[59] Winterhager, Verkündigung, 582–98.

[60] Winterhager, Verkündigung, 589.

[61] Winterhager, Verkündigung, 589.

[62] See note 58 and Fabisch/Iserloh, Dokumente, 210.

[63] Peter Wiegand, in: Netzwerke eines 'berühmten Practicus'? Was Tetzel zum erfolgreichen Ablasskommissar machte, in: Kühne/Bünz/Wiegand, Tetzel, 124–60, here: 149.

motives for doing so.[64] In any case, the vast collection of relics housed in the Castle Chapel of Wittenberg, the city's main church institution, which had been granted extensive privileges, offered an impressive number of indulgences. Still, the difference between plenary indulgences – the remission of all sins – and partial indulgences, as abundant as they may have been, remained. Only a year before denying the latest campaign access to his territories, Frederick the Wise had requested permission from the Pope to increase the number of indulgence associated with his relic collection in Wittenberg.[65]

In terms of indulgences, the campaign to support the building of St Peter's had more to offer. The campaign was announced in Leo X's bull *Sacrosanctis* of 31 March 1515,[66] and promoted plenary indulgences to a wide range of potential buyers. The bull describes in great detail the offences to be dealt with and the applicable financial contributions. The latter included temporarily redirecting to the campaign existing endowments to churches or brotherhoods. Acquirers of indulgences could select the priest to whom they made confession, and special documents instructed confessors accordingly. The offer of complete remission of all sins applied to laypeople and clerics alike, dead or alive. The *thesaurus ecclesiae*[67] referred to in the bull allowed apostolic successors, i.e. the pope and his official representatives, to administer and distribute the benefits it contained.

The bull itself did not trigger the campaign immediately since the subsequent negotiations took time. In 1516 Albrecht of Mainz was legally guaranteed half of the profits, but the operations in his

---

[64] Peter Wiegand, Marinus de Fregeno – Raimund Peraudi – Johann Tetzel. Beobachtungen zur vorreformatorischen Ablasspolitik der Wettiner, in: Rehberg, Ablasskampagnen, 305–33, here: 325.
[65] Paulus, Geschichte 3, 245.
[66] Fabisch/Iserloh, Dokumente, 212–24.
[67] Fabisch/Iserloh, Dokumente, 222–23.

territories could not start until 1517.[68] By then, the sale organized by Arcimboldi was up and running, and it is likely that Luther had already come across preachers from this leg of the campaign in 1516.[69] Apart from personal interactions, printing played an important role in publicizing the particular terms of the indulgence, as recent discoveries have shown. Summaries of the papal bull appeared in broadsides, fragments of which have been identified in both Latin and German.[70] The complete text of the German summary can be reconstructed from a quarto edition that had been considered missing since 1899,[71] but which was rediscovered in 2017.[72] To our knowledge, this summary of the bull represents the most popular printed text containing information on the terms and conditions of the offering. The German version entirely matches the Latin fragments; it can be concluded that one text was distributed in two languages and printed in at least two different formats. The title page does not survive,[73] but the header on the first page announces a summary (*Summa*) of the bull that was to offer 'the most perfect' indulgence of 'pein' and 'schuldt',[74] the German equivalents of *poena* and *culpa*. 'Pein' (translated in this edition as 'punishment')[75] refers to

---

[68] Fabisch/Iserloh, Dokumente, 211.

[69] Summing up Wolfgang Breul's argument: Volker Leppin, Das ganze Leben Buße. Der Protest gegen den Ablass im Rahmen von Luthers früher Bußtheologie, in: Rehberg, Ablasskampagnen, 523–64, here: 547, note 116.

[70] Ulrich Bubenheimer, Druckerzeugnisse aus der Leipziger Offizin Melchior Lotters d.Ä. für den von Albrecht von Brandenburg vertriebenen Petersablass und deren Funktion, in: Kühne/Bünz/Wiegand, Tetzel, 267–85.

[71] On the print cf. Bubenheimer, Petersablass, 276: 'Hier wird ein Druck vorgestellt, der gegenwärtig verschollen ist' with 277, note 51.

[72] *Dis ist ain kurtzer begriff oder Summa der macht vnnd artickel/ des aller volkommlichsten/ vnnd aller hailigsten Ablaß etc.* (BSB München, sig. Rar. 1873#Beibd. 2), digitally available at http://daten.digitale-sammlungen.de/~db/0011/bsb00110038/images/.

[73] For a suggestion on this see Bubenheimer, Petersablass, 277.

[74] *Summa*, A2r.

[75] See the first note to thesis 4 in the *95 Theses*, p. 34.

works of satisfaction imposed in life or the temporal, purifying punishments after death. 'Schuldt' (translated as 'guilt') concerns the principal dimension of human responsibility and divine acceptance or rejection. Even though the institution of penance dealt with forgiveness (or 'remission') of 'guilt', it was still possible for the required works of satisfaction – and the related 'punishment' – to remain. The bull and its publicity material might appear imprecise, but they do in fact use an established term for plenary indulgences.[76] The bull itself involves another pair of terms which have found their way into the vernacular summary by referring to indulgences and other benefits: 'indulgentias et alias gratias'.[77] The German summary uses the combination of 'ablaß' and 'gnad' frequently as a reference to the current papal offering.[78] It is not just the sermons of indulgence preachers, but also this very document which spread the word about the indulgence campaign among large numbers of people.

As a preacher, Luther began to deal with the topic of indulgences and recent developments related to them either in late 1516 or in early 1517.[79] The first relevant text survives within a sequence of sermons delivered from 1514 to 1517 and is recorded in Latin.[80] The language has been interpreted as indicating that the sermon was intended for publication;[81] it has been argued, too, that the text might not be from the municipal church in which Luther preached, but

---

[76] With reference to this text and traditions dating back to the 13th century, see Nikolaus Paulus, Johann Tetzel der Ablaßprediger, Mainz 1899, 97–98.
[77] Fabisch/Iserloh, Dokumente, 215.
[78] Cf. *Summa*, Avr, A4r, A4v.
[79] For a summary of earlier suggestions cf. WA 1, 94, note 1. A more recent appraisal has been offered by Leppin, Buße, 546–47, note 116.
[80] WA 1, 20–141, here: 94–99; for another version see WA 4, 670–74. For useful summaries and references: Erwin Iserloh, Luther zwischen Reform und Reformation. Der Thesenanschlag fand nicht statt, Münster ^{3}1966 (Katholisches Leben und Kämpfen im Zeitalter der Glaubensspaltung 23/24), 31–35.
[81] Cf. Karl Knaake in WA 1, 19.

from the chapel of the Augustinian monastery.[82] In any case, the sermon proposes that man is saved by divine grace alone and it firmly opposes indulgence teaching that undermines this fundamental understanding.[83] While the pope's motives might be 'right and true', Luther identifies the culprits as the preachers who act as 'seducers' and 'storytellers'.[84] In general, Luther summarizes penance as theologically consisting of three parts: a person's heartfelt regret (lat. *contritio cordis*), the act of confession (*confessio oris*), and satisfaction (traditionally based on works: *satisfactio operis*).[85] Even in this early sermon, Luther emphasised that all of these aspects are vital, but must be understood and applied internally, spiritually.[86]

In short, this sermon already provides the backbone of the *95 Theses* and the *Sermon on Indulgences and Grace*. Both texts start off with the established theological understanding of penance.[87] The *Sermon* names the three related components in its first point, while readers of the disputation have to combine theses 2 and 12 (or later 30, 35, 39–40, and 87) in order to identify and connect the relevant terms on the basis of their previous knowledge. Both texts proceed to deal with further scholastic statements on theoretical or practical aspects. More or less implicitly, Luther relates these to their appropriate

---

[82] Theodor Brieger, Kritische Erörterung zur neuen Luther-Ausgabe, in: Zeitschrift für Kirchengeschichte 11 (1890), 100–54, here: 122.

[83] WA 1, 98–99.

[84] WA 1, 98.

[85] Cf. the respective allusions in WA 1, 98–99. See also the note to thesis 12 of the *95 Theses*, p. 35.

[86] Esp. WA 1, 99.

[87] For a useful brief summary of the contemporary diversity of positions and arguments – including those of Thomas Aquinas and Petrus Lombardus – see Leppin, Buße, 526–34. A good translation of Lombard's relevant passages is available: Peter Lombard, The Sentences. Book 4: On the Doctrine of Signs. Translated by Giulio Silano, Toronto 2010 (Medieval Sources in Translation 48), 69–135. For the tripartite structure referred to by Luther see Lombard, Sentences, 88.

authorities: the bible, early church teachings, canon law and scholastic school traditions, reason, and every so often concludes that they derive from mere imagination. It is clear that Luther advocates a revision of later developments relating to indulgences on the basis of biblical authority.

AMORE ET STVDIO ELVCIDANDAE ueritatis hæc ſubſcripta diſputabunt̃ Vuittenbergæ, Præſidēte R. P. Martino Luther, Artiũ & S. Theologiæ Magiſtro, eiuſdemq́ ibidem lectore Ordinario. Quare petit ut qui non poſſunt uerbis præſentes nobiſcum diſceptare, agant id literis abſentes. In nomine domini noſtri Ieſu Chriſti. Amen.

i Dominus & Magiſter noſter Ieſus Chriſtus, dicendo pœnitentiã agite &c. omnem uitam fidelium, pœnitentiam eſſe uoluit.

ij Quod uerbũ pœnitentia de pœnitentia ſacramentali (.i. confeſſionis & ſatiſſactionis quæ ſacerdotum miniſterio celebratur) non poteſt intelligi.

iij Non tamen ſolã intẽdit interiorẽ: immo interior nulla eſt, niſi foris operetur uarias carnis mortificationes.

iiij Manet itaq́ pœna donec manet odium ſui (.i. pœnitentia uera intus) ſcilicet uſq́ ad introitum regni cælorum.

v Papa non uult nec poteſt, ullas pœnas remittere; præter eas, quas arbitrio uel ſuo uel canonum impoſuit.

vj Papa nõ poteſt remittere ullam culpã, niſi declarãdo & approbando remiſſam a deo. Aut certe remittẽdo caſus reſeruatos ſibi, quibus contẽptis culpa prorſus remaneret.

vij Nulli prorſus remittit deus culpam, quin ſimul eum ſubijciat humiliatum in omnibus ſacerdoti ſuo uicario.

viij Canones pœnitentiales ſolũ uiuentibus ſunt impoſiti: nihilq́ morituris, ſecundũ eoſdem debet imponi.

ix Inde bene nobis facit ſpirituſſanctus in Papa: excipiẽdo in ſuis decretis ſemper articulum mortis & neceſſitatis.

x Indocte & male faciũt ſacerdotes ij, qui morituris pœnitẽtias canonicas in purgatorium reſeruant.

xj Zizania illa de mutanda pœna Canonica in pœnã purgatorij, uidentur certe dormientibus Epiſcopis ſeminata.

xij Olim pœnæ canonicæ nõ poſt, ſed ante abſolutionem imponebantur, tanq́ tentamenta ueræ contritionis.

Ill. 3: The *95 Theses* in pamphlet format, [Basel: Adam Petri] 1517, A1v UB Basel KiAr J VI 30:1 (http://doi.org/10.3931/e-rara-273)

The *95 Theses* start off with a biblical understanding of penance, while the *Sermon on Indulgences and Grace*, as a popular piece of writing, opens with a definition of terms. One of the great advantages of the *Sermon* over the *95 Theses* is its clear structure. Its title presents two terms, which correspond to two sections into which the twenty points are organized (see the black border in the table below). The word 'grace' appears once only in the text (in point 13), but it is highlighted by the title and is present in the line of argument. The combination of terms provides a striking response to the vernacular summary of the papal bull.[88] At the same time, the formal structure of the *Sermon* corresponds to the Latin and German *Summa* in its length and division into around twenty points. Since the German *Summa* must, as things stand, be considered the most popular printed text in the campaign, the even more popular *Sermon* might be considered an answer to the promotional publicity of the bull's summaries.[89] While Luther's *Sermon* adheres in important aspects of its format and content to the most widely distributed printed tracts of the campaign, his own classification of it as a *Sermon* gives it a spiritual and pastoral framework.

A summary of its contents (below) illustrates its structure and highlights how Luther introduces particular elements of scholastic teaching traditions, questions their authority, and compares them with what he understands the corresponding biblical foundation to be. The first column lists the paragraph of the *Sermon* followed by

---

[88] See note 78.

[89] Ulrich Bubenheimer, Reliquienfest und Ablass in Halle. Albrecht von Brandenburgs Werbemedien und die Gegenschriften Karlstadts und Luthers, in: Stefan Oehmig (ed.), Buchdruck und Buchkultur im Wittenberg der Reformationszeit, Leipzig 2015 (Schriften der Stiftung Luthergedenkstätten 21), 71–100, reconstructed in great detail Luther's and Karlstadt's reactions to Albrecht of Mainz's offers of indulgences in Halle between 1520 and 1522. He classifies the Archbishop's prior publications as 'promotional advertisements' ('Werbung'), 81–82, 90. Bubenheimer's analysis reinforces the interpretation given above.

the topics, the theological doctrines in the scholastic tradition, the authorities according to Luther, and finally Luther's own position. The shaded area accentuates the *Sermon*'s positive message and Luther's advice.

§	Topics	Scholastic tradition	Authorities	Luther's position
1.	Penitence	Comprises (1) Contrition (2) Confession (3) Satisfaction	Unscriptural, unpatristic	
2.	Indulgence	Requires 1 and 2, refers to 3		
3.	Satisfaction	Combines acts of a) Prayer b) Fasting c) Almsgiving		
4.	Indulgence and satisfaction	Indulgences partially reduce the works imposed		
5. – 6.	Indulgence and 'punishment'	Controversial whether indulgences reduce divine 'punishment'	Unscriptural 'opinion' (6)	Biblical: contrition and works come from genuine motivation (6)
7. – 8.				Biblical: divinely imposed 'punishment' leads to contrition (7) and is only partially understood by man (8)
9.		Specification of divine punishments	Fictional 'prattle'	Divinely imposed 'punishment' is beneficial for man
10.		The total amount of (temporal) punishment might exceed an individual's lifetime	'empty words' and 'fabrication'	Biblical: God and the 'holy church' are moderate

§	Topics	Scholastic tradition	Authorities	Luther's position
11.		Canon law once related mortal sins to seven years of penance		Christians have to be moderate
12.		Sins without satisfaction during one's lifetime lead to purgatory (or demand indulgence)	'without foundation and proof'	
13.	Grace	Satisfaction is necessary for the forgiveness of sins	'error'	God's forgiveness is free and expects only personal progress
14. – 16.	Good works			Indulgences encourage human idleness (14). Good works have to be done 'for God's sake' (15); they should first help the needy nearby, then the local church, and only as a last resort the church in Rome or elsewhere
17. – 20.	Summary	Indulgences rescue souls from purgatory (18)	'impossible to prove', 'opinions', undecided by the church (18)	Suggested strategies include: don't purchase indulgences (16); don't hinder indulgence sales (17); encourage personal 'punishment', charitable deeds, and prayers for others (18). This advice is biblical (19), steeped in Christian tradition, and not heretical (20).

When we compare the *95 Theses* with the *Sermon von Ablass und Gnade*,[90] it is clear that they differ in their target readership, their publicity, their intertextual references and, of course, their specific aims. The *Sermon* was conceived above all as a popular piece of writing.[91] In fact, it is Luther's first vernacular publication with mass appeal. The initial editions were produced by Johann Rhau-Grunenberg in Wittenberg, who came out with at least four of them in 1518.[92] In the same year, printing houses in Leipzig, Nuremberg, Augsburg, and Basel followed suit. Within less than one year, at least 14 editions had appeared. Public demand continued in 1519 and 1520 with at least another nine editions from Wittenberg, Leipzig, Augsburg, Basel, and Breslau. A version in Low German was published in Braunschweig in 1518.[93] Otto Clemen concluded that

---

[90] WA 1, 239–46. Martin Luther, Deutsch-Deutsche Studienausgabe, 1: Glaube und Leben, ed. by Dietrich Korsch, Leipzig 2012, 1–11 (translated by Johannes Schilling). For the English translation see below, pp. 1–31.

[91] This is explained primarily given its status as a 'new form of theological writing' by Andrew Pettegree, The Reformation as a Media Event, in: Archiv für Reformationsgeschichte 108 (2017), 126–33, here: 126.

[92] For the editions identified and mentioned here, see Benzing/Claus, Lutherbibliographie 1, 16–19, nos 90–114; 2, Baden-Baden 1994 (Bibliotheca bibliographica Aureliana 143), 28–30, nos 90–114. Recent summaries are provided by Johannes Schilling, Ein Sermon von Ablass und Gnade (1518) – Historische und theologische Aspekte, in: Irene Dingel and Henning P. Jürgens (eds), Meilensteine der Reformation. Schlüsseldokumente der frühen Wirksamkeit Martin Luthers, Gütersloh 2014, 108–12, here: 108–10, and Claudine Moulin, Ein Sermon von Ablass und Gnade (1518) – Materialität: Dynamik und Transformation, in: Dingel/Jürgens, Meilensteine, 113–19, here: 113–14. See also the print history of the Taylorian copies in this edition, pp. xxxix–lii.

[93] Suggestions about who was responsible for the translation and print will be given by Ulrich Bubenheimer, Thomas Müntzer in seinem vor- und frühreformatorischen Umfeld in Braunschweig, in: Birgit Hoffmann and Dieter Rammler (eds), Themen – Akteure – Medien der Reformationszeit, Wolfenbüttel 2018 (Quellen und Beiträge zur Geschichte der Evangelisch-lutherischen Landeskirche in Braunschweig).

the public success of the *Sermon* killed off the *95 Theses*.[94] More recently, it has been argued that the *Sermon* actually brought the theses to life.[95] Indeed, some of the contents of the theses were moved into the more popular format of the *Sermon*. Still, Luther's own intention was to stop further circulation of his theses without explanatory comments. His *Resolutiones* were an academic step in this direction, the *Sermon* a popular one. On 5 March 1518 Luther announced to Scheurl in Nuremberg that he hoped to publish a 'vernacular booklet on indulgences, in order to suppress those theses which have spread so widely'.[96] This reference is important in determining the *terminus post quem* for our *Sermon*. Older scholarship dated the compilation of the *Sermon* to the previous year and saw in the remark to Scheurl another publication project that remained unrealized.[97] However, two other letters clearly refer to the *Sermon*. In one, Luther reports to Spalatin on the topic of indulgences that the Bishop of Brandenburg 'strongly' opposed the publication, printing, and sale 'of a popular sermon'.[98] The document is undated and has been placed partially by conjecture,[99] partially with good reason[100] at least a fortnight after Luther's message to Scheurl. The second relevant letter marks the *terminus ante quem* for the *Sermon*. On 8 May 1518 Luther writes to his teacher Jodokus Trutfetter in Erfurt that he assumes he would not like the 'popular sermon' he has produced.[101] The timeframe from the first week of March to the first

---

[94] Otto Clemen (ed.), Luthers Werke in Auswahl. Unter Mitwirkung von Albert Leitzmann, 1, Bonn 1912, 10.

[95] Schilling, Sermon, 108.

[96] WA.Br 1, 152.

[97] Cf. Karl Knaake in WA 1, 239. Knaake's suggestion was strongly criticised by contemporary scholars soon after the WA's publication. The best discussion of the relevant primary sources is still Brieger, Erörterung, 112–25.

[98] WA.Br 1, 162.

[99] WA.Br 1, 161. Following this Clemen, Werke, 10.

[100] Brieger, Erörterung, 124–25, note 3.

[101] WA.Br 1, 170.

week of May is narrowed down even further when we look at the *Sermon* itself. Several points relate to a publication[102] that had arrived in Wittenberg by the middle of March.[103] Point 9 of the *Sermon* rejects a terminological distinction that had been discussed in a series of disputation theses at Frankfurt an der Oder.[104] These were a response to Luther's *95 Theses*; the actual disputation involved Johannes Tetzel, who was employed by Albrecht of Mainz in his indulgence campaign.[105] That disputation also raises the question as to who might have to be considered a 'heretic',[106] before quoting from Luther's theses at great length. The *Sermon*'s final point refers to this ('I may well be branded a heretic by people'). Some of Luther's letters and one other sermon suggest that printed versions of the relevant disputation theses became available in Wittenberg between 17 and 19 March 1518.[107] This, together with Luther's absence from Wittenberg for his journey to Heidelberg from mid-April[108] to mid-May,[109] means that the *Sermon* has to be dated between mid-March

---

[102] For Nikolaus Paulus' references to this cf. Clemen, Werke, 10. In more detail see Brieger, Erörterung, 121–22.

[103] Cf. Brieger, Erörterung, 121–22, and Fabisch/Iserloh, Dokumente, 314.

[104] See the note to the translation of §9 in this edition, p. 15. The relevant passages can be found in Fabisch/Iserloh, Dokumente, 331, no. 49. The context is explained by Martin Ohst, Pflichtbeichte. Untersuchungen zum Bußwesen im Hohen und Späten Mittelalter, Tübingen 1995 (Beiträge zur historischen Theologie 89), 77, note 106.

[105] Fabisch/Iserloh, Dokumente, 310–11. On Tetzel see recently Kühne/Bünz/Wiegand, Tetzel.

[106] Fabisch/Iserloh, Dokumente, 326, no. 21.

[107] See note 104. After prints had become locally available, students burned them. Luther publicly opposed this action in his sermon on 19 March 1518, WA 1, 277 (the sermon from 17 March 1518, WA 1, 267–73, bears no reference). In his letters the incident is mentioned to Johannes Lang in Erfurt on 21 March, WA.Br 1, 155, and to Trutfetter WA.Br 1, 170–71.

[108] WA.Br. 1, 166.

[109] WA.Br. 1, 173.

and mid-April 1518.[110] Bearing in mind, further, the fact that Tetzel reports in his next publication, the *Vorlegung*, that Luther's *Sermon* was published 'yn der fasten iungst',[111] which lasted from 17 February to 3 April,[112] one has to conclude the *Sermon* was completed and published in the second half of March 1518.

To summarize the relationship between the *Sermon* and the *95 Theses*, one might describe them as contrasting and complementary. They differ in their mix of scholarly and popular elements, but each offers a combination of both. While the *Sermon* introduces academic distinctions only to refute them, the *95 Theses* present popular criticism of indulgence theory and practice to learned and ecclesiastically aware readers.[113] The *95 Theses* finish off with a sequence of popular concerns and complaints (theses 81–89, along with the concluding thesis 90). Another clearly defined sequence (theses 42–51) deals with what should be taught to Christians (including the laity). The *Sermon* has a corresponding section (points 15–17) which includes specific pieces of advice. Both texts are based on the assumption that church doctrine on indulgences has not been finalised: the *95 Theses* form part of an exchange on the topic that might be described – socially and structurally – as top-down, while the *Sermon*'s contribution is bottom-up. Another text that Luther sent to Albrecht of Mainz along with his letter and the *95 Theses* should be mentioned in this context. This is a *Tractatus de*

---

[110] 17 March 1518 accordingly marks the *terminus post quem*, and not the 'terminus ante quem für die abfassung des sermons' as Clemen, Werke, 11, had it.

[111] Fabisch/Iserloh, Dokumente, 340.

[112] Brieger, Erörterung, 125, note 1.

[113] Reaffirming Winterhager (see note 49) this was emphasised by Thomas Kaufmann, Luthers 95 Thesen in ihrem historischen Zusammenhang, in: Thomas Kaufmann, Der Anfang der Reformation, Tübingen 2012 (Spätmittelalter, Humanismus, Reformation 67), 166–84, here: 169–70.

Indulgentiis,[114] a work which might include excerpts from earlier sermons edited and expanded for an academic audience. The text is interesting, since it contains a statement by Luther of at least one of the arguments attributed to the laity in the *95 Theses*.[115] Tetzel's name does not appear in any of the texts by Luther we have mentioned, although some passages in them refute statements attributed to Tetzel.[116] The *95 Theses* and the accompanying letter to Albrecht of Mainz go beyond the main public protagonists and engage at a senior level with the organisation of the current indulgence campaign by referring directly to instructions in the contents of an official document provided for personnel involved in the campaign.[117] This *Instructio summaria ad Subcommissarios, Penetentiarios et Confessores*, used by Albrecht of Mainz, is a follow-up to related documents of earlier campaigns and was printed by Melchior Lotter in Leipzig.[118] By alluding to the text of the *Instructio summaria*, Luther challenges a scholarly public to make a judgement on the legitimacy of Albrecht's campaign and demands that the Archbishop

---

114 WA.Br 12, 5–10 with useful introductory remarks WA.Br 12, 2–5. For good summaries see Iserloh, Thesenanschlag, 35–40, and Leppin, Buße, 556–60.

115 Cf. thesis 82 with WA.Br 12, 6: *Alioquin crudelis est Papa, si hoc miseris animabus non concedit gratis, quod potest pro pecunia missa ad ecclesiam concedere* ('Or else the pope is being cruel if he does not grant to wretched souls for free what he can grant for money contributed to the church').

116 See notes 104–106 above and the notes to §9 of the *Sermon* and to thesis 75 of the *95 Theses* in the present edition.

117 Cf. the notes to theses 20, 28, 33, 35, 37, 53, 67, 73, 84, and 88 in the present edition. The text is introduced and edited by Fabisch/Iserloh, Dokumente, 246–93. For translated parts see Hillerbrand, Reformation, 14–18.

118 Fabisch/Iserloh, Dokumente, 254. The best way to study the references in the *95 Theses* alluding to the *Instructio summaria* is to consult the edition of Silvester Prierias' reaction to Luther, which quotes widely from the theses: Fabisch/Iserloh, Dokumente, 56–106. For the latest corrections to the earlier *Instructiones confessorum*, which were used in both Mainz and Magdeburg, see Bubenheimer, Petersablass, 267–71.

either withdraw the campaign or correct the contents of the document.[119] One might wonder whether this expectation was realistic or proportionate. Bearing in mind the territorial opposition to the campaigns and increasing popular criticism of indulgences (of which church representatives were aware), one might have expected a variety of reactions in the episcopacy at the time. Indeed, an early document from November 1517 suggests that Adolf of Anhalt, Bishop of Merseburg, on behalf of his territorial Duke, George of Saxony, publicly supported Luther's positions.[120]

As for the wider historical repercussions of the events set out above, the *95 Theses* reached Rome via at least three channels: Albrecht of Mainz together with his advisors, the Dominican Order around Tetzel,[121] and eventually Eck. To some extent this outcome is in keeping with Luther's aim of instigating a debate which would have practical relevance. The *95 Theses* and, more precisely, the way in which they were publicized, urged clarification on fundamental and topical questions. Within the course of one year they succeeded: on 9 November 1518 a papal bull summarized and reinforced a number of the teachings Luther had questioned.[122] By this time, of course, the debate had moved on. The *Sermon on Indulgences and Grace* was a major popular factor in this. Today it allows readers to gain a sense of the very text from which numerous contemporary readers formed their first impressions of Luther. By progressing from the *Sermon* to the *95 Theses* we gain an awareness of some of the implications which developed from it, including on papal power, biblical authority, and the participation of the laity. At the same time, the *Sermon* can be used as a starting-point to read some of Luther's other

---

[119] WA.Br 1, 112; for a partial translation see Hillerbrand, Reformation, 26–27.

[120] Kaufmann, Thesen, 173 with note 37. Winterhager, Verkündigung, 591, identifies political interests behind the bishop's actions and announces further publications on it.

[121] For a summary cf. Fabisch/Iserloh, Dokumente, 31.

[122] Denzinger/Hünermann, Kompendium, 452–53, no. 1447–49.

early printed sermons, which deal with a variety of subjects that were of immense practical relevance to Christians five centuries ago.[123]

[123] Examples from the following years include: *Ein Sermon vom Sakrament der Buße* (1519); *Ein Sermon von dem hochwürdigen Sakrament des heiligen wahren Leichnams Christi und von den Bruderschaften* (1519); *Ein Sermon von der Bereitung zum Sterben* (1519); *Ein Sermon von dem heiligen hochwürdigen Sakrament der Taufe* (1519); *Sermon von dem Wucher* (1519); *Ein Sermon von dem Neuen Testament, das ist von der heiligen Messe* (1520). For a comprehensive list see Kurt Aland, Hilfsbuch zum Lutherstudium, Bielefeld [4]1996, 160–61.

2. The Taylorian Copies

The *Sermon on Indulgences and Grace* was the first big publicity coup for Martin Luther. Printers in Leipzig, Nuremberg, Augsburg, and Basel followed, in quick succession, the lead publication in Wittenberg. There are at least seven copies of the *Sermon* in Oxford, five as part of the 84 multi-item collection of 'Tractatus Lutherani' (Tr.Luth.),[124] two in the Taylor Institution Library.[125] Looking through the hastily printed, well-thumbed, often annotated, and widely travelled pamphlets, the excitement of this explosive time in print production comes to life. The following chapter tells the story of the materiality of the *Sermon* from production to acquisition through a study of the two Taylorian copies.[126]

2.1 Production

Henrike Lähnemann

The two Taylorian copies, one produced by Pamphilus Gengenbach in Basel and one by Valentin Schumann in Leipzig, reflect the momentum of Reformation printing in different ways. The *Sermon*

[124] Most of the Tr.Luth. pamphlets were bought by the Bodleian Library in 1818 from the collection of the Augsburg Professor Johannes Gottlob May who arranged them in roughly chronological order. All Reformation pamphlets in Oxford are included in Michael A. Pegg, A Catalogue of German Reformation Pamphlets (1516–1546) in Libraries of Great Britain and Ireland, Baden-Baden 1973. The *Sermon* copies are listed on p. 193.
[125] Benzing/Claus, Lutherbibliographie, nos 90–103. For the online version of the Verzeichnis deutschsprachiger Drucke use http://gateway-bayern.de/VD16+L+ followed by the four-digit VD16 number, e.g. 6268 for the Basel print in the Taylorian and 6270 for the Leipzig print.
[126] On the topicality of the debate about materiality cf. the two new series *Kulturen des Sammelns* ed. by the HAB Wolfenbüttel and *New Directions in Book History* http://www.springer.com/series/14749.

was an ideal test case for the new format: it required only six pages of text, which meant that it could be fitted onto one quire in quarto format with space for a title page and a colophon. Both printers decided to concentrate on the text and to give neither the place of publication nor their own name, but the typeface and the woodcut decoration make it possible to attribute both editions with reasonable certainty. The two printers developed this basic format in different ways.

Pamphilus Gengenbach: Popular Printing

> Martin Luther, *Sermon von Ablass und Gnade*
> [Basel: Pamphilus Gengenbach 1518]
> Title: (E)Jn Sermon oder Predig || von dem ablasz vnd gnade || durch den wirdigen docto=||rem Martinum Luther Augu||stiner zu wittenbergk ge=||macht vnd gepre||diget.|| + ||
> Impressum: Getruckt nach Christ geburt Tausent || fünffhundert vnd ym achtzehēdē Jar.||
> 4° A4 Quire signatures Aij, Aiij. Types: A 2, T 2D. Cross,
> Taylor Institution Library, Arch. 8° G. 1518 (5)
> Woodcuts: letter E and Z, floral borders, man approaching a church, deposition from the cross
> WA 1, 241, no. M; Benzing/Claus no. 102; VD16 L 6268

Basel was home to Humanist printing at the highest level and established itself as one of the foremost centres of Reformation printing: Erasmus had worked with the printer Froben on his New Testament which was published in Basel in 1516, and it was one of the places where the *95 Theses* were printed in 1517.[127] But the *Sermon*, the first German Lutheran print to be published there,[128]

---

[127] On copies in Oxford of examples of the Erasmus-Froben collaboration cf. https://magdlibs.com/2015/02/04/erasmus-froben-and-holbein/.

[128] Kerstin Prietzel, Pamphilus Gengenbach, Drucker zu Basel (um 1480–1525), in: Archiv für Geschichte des Buchwesens 52 (1999), 229–461, here 336.

comes from a popular press rather than from an academic publisher. The printer was Pamphilus Gengenbach, a proponent of the Reformation from the very beginning, and an established printer-author, writing Shrovetide plays and poems, and publishing popular literature as well as topical Latin texts.

Gengenbach had already exploited the indulgence debate for popular, indeed humorous, effect. Around 1513, he wrote a satirical poem about *durre ritter* (poor knights who supplement their income by robbery) which he published himself as a broadside (single-leaf print) masquerading as a letter of indulgence. This promises those who support the knights that they will get as much remission for their sins as if they had put the money in the collecting tin in front of Basel Minster (*wer jn git zerung vber nacht / sie vnd ire pferd wol entpfacht / Der soll den ablossz han / als hett ers jnn die kist geton / Die zu Basell vor dem munster stat / den ablosz das concilia bestetiget hat*) and confirms that these poor knights will all go straight to heaven.[129]

Gengenbach did sign some of the texts he published, e.g. Luther's *Apologetica responsio contra dogmata* which he published in the same year as the *Sermon.*[130] There he signs with the programmatic Latin statement that

ra docuerit.
VERITATI CONSECRATVM,
Basileę apud Pamphilũ Gengenbachium
Mẽse Augusto, AN, M, D,XVIII,

Ill. 4: Bodleian Library, Tr. Luth. 1 (18), A4r

[129] Prietzel, Gengenbach, no. 5. Digital copy at https://www.e-rara.ch/doi/10.3931/e-rara-2017. On the biography of Gengenbach, cf. Christoph Reske, Die Buchdrucker des 16. und 17. Jahrhunderts im deutschen Sprachgebiet. Auf der Grundlage des gleichnamigen Werkes von Josef Benzing. 2nd revised and enlarged edition, Wiesbaden 2015 (Beiträge zum Buch- und Bibliothekswesen 51), 71.

[130] Basel: Pamphilus Gengenbach 1518, Prietzel, Gengenbach, no. 43; VD16 W 3070 is used in the Bodleian Library copy, Tr. Luth. 1 (18). Digital copy at http://doi.org/10.3931/e-rara-261.

it is *DEDICATED TO TRUTH at Basel by Pamphilus Gengenbach in August 1518* (ill. 4).

By contrast, he keeps the *Sermon* unsigned, preferring to highlight on the title-page, in large blackletter font, the celebrity author, the *wirdige doctor Martinus Luther Augustiner*, and the place where the *Sermon* was originally composed and preached: *zu wittenbergk gemacht vnd gepredigET* (ill. 5). This title-page is a hotchpotch of catchy words, decorative elements, and clues to the text's religious content.

Ein Sermon oder Predig
von dem ablaß vnd gnade
durch den wirdigen docto-
rem Martinum Luther Augu
stiner zu wittenbergk ge-
macht vnd gepre
diget.

Apologetica respon sio
contra dogmata, quę in M. Io.
Syluiũ Egranum a calum
niatoribus inuul-
gata sunt.

E R
Impietas, ē ad impietatis crimē eē mutũ.

Ill. 5: Taylorian, Arch. 8°G.1518(5)

Ill. 6: Bodleian Library, Tr. Luth. 1 (18)

Other publications from the same year are surrounded by four woodcut borders which neatly frame the title; for example, for the *Apologetica responsio* (ill. 6) he used two of four blocks depicting cunning women (above: Delilah cutting off Samson's hair; below: Phyllis riding Aristotle) and two decorative side borders which come from a different set but are at least of exactly the right length.

Ill. 7: UB Basel, UBH FM1 IX 18, A2v (e-rara)

By contrast, Gengenbach's print of the *Sermon* features two decorative floral border elements which seem to have been cut down from woodcuts, since they only extend halfway up the page. They look very similar to the decorative borders used around the same time by Gengenbach for his print of a verse legend; these were obviously leftovers from a page-sized woodcut framed by floral borders and Swiss coats of arms (ill. 7).[131] For the *Sermon* they might have been further cut down to avoid the local element of the coat of arms and preserve the anonymity of the print.

To compensate for the fact that the borders went only halfway up, a woodcut initial 'E' from a Roman typeface is used as the first letter of the title, sitting incongruously with the black letter font of the following text, which itself runs on in the same size rather than having a smaller font size for the subtitle. This 'E', whose middle stroke is used by a putto as mouthpiece for drinking or possibly blowing a trumpet, can be seen in its proper place as part of a Latin text-block in the *Apologetica responsio* on A1v where it opens the sentence *En tibi arbitrium meum* (ill. 8).

N TIBI AR
um de dogmat
Sylui ſuauiſſ.P
ſub iudiciũ ecc
rũ tui (vt d'r) ſu
loq̃ cũ timore
Secũdo.Oĩa vera credo, & fere

Ill. 8: Bodleian Library, Tr. Luth. 1 (18), A1v

---

[131] Kunz Kistener, *Ein hübsch lesen und grosz wunderzeichen von dem heiligen zwölffbotten sant Jacob und zweien Jacobs brüdern*, VD16 K 2571.

Another letter of the same Roman alphabet is used for the initial 'Z' of the first paragraph of the *Sermon* (A1v).

Ein Sermon oder Predig võ dem ab
lasz vnd gnade durch den wirdigen do
ctorem Martinum Luther Augusti-
ner zu wittenbergk gemacht vnd ge-
prediget.

Z Vdem ersten söllend jr wissen/das etzlich
new lerer/als Magister Sen.S.Tomas
vnd jre volger geben der büsz drey theil.
Nemlich die rew/die beicht/die gnůgthů-
ung/vnd wie wol diser vnderscheid nach
jrer meinung/schwerlich oder auch gar ni
chts/gegründet erfunden wirt yn der heiligẽ geschryfft/no

F. MARTINVS E-
LEVTHERIVS
AVGVST. SVO IO.
SYLVIO S.

N TIBI ARBITRIVM ME-
um de dogmatibꝰ tuis, vt voluisti mi
Sylui suauiss. Primũ placet, ꝙ omnia
sub iudiciũ ecclesię, in primis ordina
rij tui (vt d'r) submittis. Nã vera etiã
loqͥ cũ timore oportet in Ecclesia dei:
Secũdo. Oĩa vera credo, & fere ipsemetiã diu & legi

Ill. 9: Taylorian, Arch. 8°G.1518 (5), A1v, cf. facsimile F4

Ill. 10: Bodleian Library, Tr. Luth. 1 (18), A1v

The small woodcut in the middle of the bottom half of the page shows a man with rosary in hand heading towards a chapel – an example of 'handwerklicher Durchschnittsstil'[132] and also of the conventional piety of set prayers and church attendance, which sits slightly at odds with the fiery tone of the *Sermon*. This is complemented on the reverse by a large woodcut of the deposition from the cross (A4v, cf. facsimile F16).[133] It concentrates on the grief of Mary who is the middle of the composition flanked by John the Evangelist and Mary Magdalene and surrounded by further elements of the passion such as the crown of thorns in the bottom right-hand corner, dramatically highlighted by being in white cut out of the black background. This is a popular late medieval devotional image *par excellence*, inviting devout readers to encounter the passion personally through the compassion of Mary. Even though no direct model has been identified (nor any other print where it is used), it

---

[132] Hans Koegler, Die illustrierten Erbauungsbücher, Heiligenlegenden und geistlichen Auslegungen im Basler Buchdruck der ersten Hälfte des XVI. Jahrhunderts: mit Ausschluss der Postillen, Passionate, Evangelienbücher und Bibeln (Basler Zeitschrift für Geschichte und Altertumskunde 39), 1940, 53–157, here: 145, E. 12.

[133] Koegler, Erbauungsbücher, 126.

must have been a recycled piece used previously for other devotional purposes. Koegler lists it in his appendix among 'vereinzelten Basler Bücherholzschnitte erbaulichen oder hagiographischen Inhalts zwischen 1500 und 1550'; they tend to be in folio format, designed to be glued on wood and hung on the wall. The combination of the man with the rosary heading for church on the title and the composition, which focuses on the passion of Christ and the suffering of Mary, show how Pamphilus Gengenbach read the *Sermon* – or at least how he thought he could market it best: not as a piece of polemical writing, still less as part of an academic debate, but as a devotional text that encouraged readers to start their quest for the remission of sins by looking at their own piety rather than by acquiring it through money. In a way, the broadside becomes an alternative to buying indulgences: a self-help pamphlet rather than a time-off voucher for purgatory.

As an established printer with experience in the market for vernacular texts, Pamphilus Gengenbach could respond quickly to changing trends. The *Sermon* was printed as a so-called 'Zwitterdruck' or hybrid edition: when Gengenbach had finished printing one side of the sheet (title, last page, A2v and A3r), he must have realised that he was on to a good thing and could sell more copies. The reverse of the broadsheet (A1v–A2r and A3v–A4r)[134] was therefore printed in a larger print run than the front side; the front page then needed to be re-typeset to complete the extra copies since the standing type had been disassembled after a set number of impressions. This means that the reverse of the broadside is identical, the front only nearly identical – thanks to the digitised editions linked to the VD16, it is possible to play 'Spot the difference'.[135]

---

[134] Cf. 'Fold your own pamphlet' on the Taylorian blog: A1r, A2v, A3r, A4v.

[135] VD16 L 6268 lists six copies; the corrections in vol. 2 of Benzing/Claus (1994), no. 102 six further copies, including the Taylorian, based on Prietzel, Pamphilus Gengenbach, no. 39, 277 (who also gives shelfmarks for all

The Taylorian copy features different line breaks on A2v and A3r and one hyphen fewer in the title than the copies from the other batch. In addition, on the otherwise identical reverse, the quire signature Aij shows up. The whole print run must have been issued before 4 September 1518, since Capito mentions the Basel print as known in a letter to Luther.[136] In October 1518, a Latin translation based on one of the Gengenbach editions was included in the first Complete Works of Luther, published by Froben together with the Latin *Sermo de poenitentia* which Gengenbach had published more or less simultaneously with the *Sermon* in 1518.[137]

Gengenbach's edition thus shows us how an astute printer-author adapted quickly in the developing religious debate to a newly emerging audience of avid readers in the vernacular.

Ill. 11: Right-hand border of the other batch of the hybrid edition VD16 L 6267 UB Basel, FM1 X 16:16, http://dx.doi.org/10.3931/e-rara-398

---

copies). VD 16 L 6267 lists three copies; Benzing/Claus no. 101 two further copies, based on Prietzel, Pamphilus Gengenbach, no. 40. She thinks that the batch including the Taylorian copy was the first batch to be printed, while the WA 1 lists it as the second batch. The additional quire signature Aij in the VD16 L 6268 edition seems to support this sequence of printing.

[136] WA.Br 1, no. 91, 198.

[137] There is a copy in Oxford in the Bodleian Library, Tr.Luth. 86 (7).

Valentin Schumann: An Annotated Copy

Martin Luther, Sermon von Ablass und Gnade
[Leipzig: Valentin Schumann 1518]
Eyn Sermon || von dem Ablaß vnnd || gnade durch den || wirdigeñ doctorñ Mar||tinū Luther Augus||tiner zu Wittē||bergk ge=|| macht.||
Impressum: Getruckt Nach Christ geburt Tausent||funffhundert vñ ym achczehenden Jar.||
[4] fol. Quire signatures Aij, Aiij. Taylor Institution Library, Arch. 8° G. 1518 (6); Woodcut borders; marginalia from several hands. WA 1, 241, no. F; Benzing/Claus no. 96;[138] Reske, Buchdrucker, 559 (Schumann); VD16 L 6270

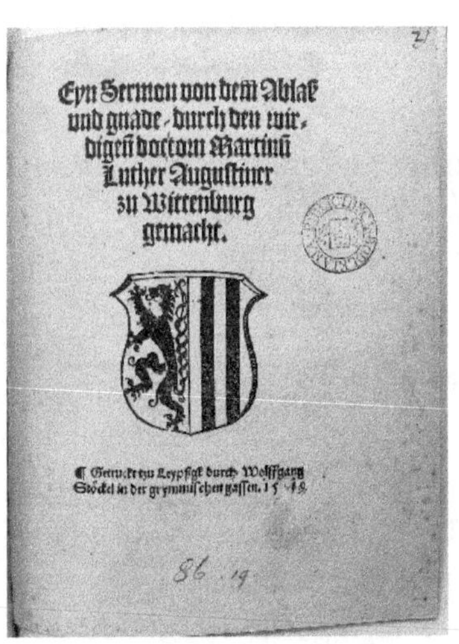
Eyn Sermon von dem Ablaß
vnd gnade / durch den wir-
digeñ doctorm Martinū
Luther Augustiner
zu Wittenburg
gemacht.

¶ Getruckt tzu Leypsigk durch Wolffgang
Stöckel in der grymmischen gassen. 15 19.

Ill. 12: Bodleian Library, Tr.Luth. 1 (18), A4r

Leipzig had several printers sharing fonts and taking up the same texts in quick succession. Valentin Schumann and Wolfgang Stöckel between them printed four editions of the *Sermon* in 1518. Stöckel and a third printer, Melchior Lotter the Elder, then reissued them in 1519 and even 1520. Only one of these editions bears the name of a printer, the 1519 edition by Stöckel which features a large coat of arms and a full credit to printer, time, and place (ill. 11). By then it had already become a piece of history – this can be seen on the title page of the

[138] VD16 lists copies in Erfurt, MinB; Frankfurt/Main, Bibliothek der Philosophisch-Theologischen Hochschule St. Georgen; SUB Göttingen; UB Heidelberg; UB Leipzig; UB Würzburg; Wittenberg, Evangelisches Predigerseminar; HAB Wolfenbüttel; Benzing/Claus no. 96 further copies in Cambridge TrinityC and Kopenhagen KglB but not the Taylorian copy.

Bodleian copy (Tr.Luth. 86 (19)) which had the year erased, presumably to date the *Sermon* back to the time of the first publication in 1518. Another contemporary hand has in turn rubbed out the fake date and reinstated the '19' in the year (ill. 12).

In the course of a year, the debate had galloped on and the Leipzig printers were crucial in this: Melchior Lotter produced the only edition of Tetzel's German answer to the *Sermon*, a 'Rebuttal' made by Tetzel as the Order of Preachers' inquisitor of heretics 'against a presumptuous sermon of twenty erroneous articles concerning papal indulgences and grace' (*Vorlegung … wyder eynen vormessen Sermon von tzwentzig irrigen Artickeln Bebstlichen ablas vnd gnade belangende*).[139] This constitutes in fact another publication of the *Sermon* in Leipzig in 1518, since Tetzel quotes each of Luther's articles in full before marking it as wrong and dangerous. It runs to four quires in the same format as Luther's *Sermon*, i.e. four times the length. Luther countered this in his follow-up publication 'A vindication of the sermon concerning the Pope's indulgences and grace' (*Ein Freiheit des Sermons päpstlichen Ablass und Gnad belangend*), this time running to two quires and numerous editions, even if it did not prove quite as popular as the first pithy publication in the debate.

Because of the identical font and anonymous publication of most of the pamphlets, it is hard to determine which printer published which edition, but taking the dated and signed Stöckel edition as a starting point, it seems likely that three of the 1518 editions were also printed by him, while the fourth, of which the Taylorian copy is an example, was printed by Valentin Schumann. This in turn points to Schumann as publisher of the edition VD16 L5451 in the Leipzig signature type, a copy of which is in the Taylorian, Arch.8°G.1523 (43/2), since it shares a border element with the Schumann print of the *Sermon* (cf. ill. 2). The watermark (bull's head with eyes, nostrils, and double-

[139] VD16 L 6269. English translation and introduction by Dewey Weiss Kramer, An Occasional Publication of the Pitts Theology Library, Atlanta 2012 online via http://pitts.emory.edu/files/Documents/Tetzel.pdf.

contoured staff with six-petalled flower above), though in itself hardly distinctive, is also clearly identical in both pamphlets.

But what makes the Taylorian copy special is not so much that it has the decorative border which Valentin Schumann provided and which – other than in the Basel edition discussed previously – fits like a glove around the well spaced and elegantly laid out title page. Rather it is the evidence of a close engagement with the text by more than one reader from the sixteenth to the eighteenth centuries. There are annotations in at least three different hands, marking up the text and providing copious marginalia on the title page and the empty end-paper. As is often the case, once a first reader had started making comments, others followed suit. The first layer of comments seems intended to highlight portions of text by underlining and marking them up in the margins. Reader one used brownish ink simply to mark up the structure, underlining all numbers and then key words to bring out the main lines of the argument. An example is §2 (A1v) where *Czum andern*, *nycht*, *das ist*, and *sundern* are underlined; applied to the English translation this would run: '<u>§2.</u> They say that indulgences do <u>not</u> take away the first or second parts, <u>that is</u>, contrition or confession, <u>but</u> the third, namely satisfaction.' This would have also have helped when the text was read out loud (cf. 'How to Read the *Sermon*').

The same hand also marks particularly pertinent paragraphs by bracketing them in the margin and twice placing an additional capital 'N' for *nota* – pay attention! – next to it. This concerns §6 where 'N' is next to the passage in which Luther firmly states his conviction that Scripture does not prove that divine righteousness desires punishment and instead argues for heartfelt contrition. In §13 'N' relates to the mistaken belief that man could make good his sins given that God forgives everything for free through grace. The 'unscheczliche gnad' is underlined in darker ink – by either a second reader or the first annotator returning to the passage at a later stage. This dark ink is also used to highlight the powerful address to the reader at the end of §16: let lazy Christians buy indulgences, and follow your own path.

This is very much in line with what happened to other Reformation pamphlets where reader engagement tended to start with basic annotations of the text. Pen trials also seem to belong to this early phase since they were cut when the pamphlet was bound into a collective volume to preserve it as the glue strip on the title-page confirms; some show signs of the accidental rubbing and grime consistent with the fold across the middle which suggests that the pamphlet was carried around and repeatedly consulted before being eventually shelved. Aside from squiggles and several stabs at writing a Latin phrase starting with *memini*, this early hand writes *domine non sum d[ignus]* ('Lord, I am not worthy [to receive you but only say the word and I shall be healed]') from the mass – an appropriate response not only to the offer of bread and wine at the Eucharist but also to the offer of salvation through grace which the *Sermon* promises.

The bulk of the marginalia - long lists of proverbs which were added on the title page, the spare space on A4r, and the lower part of A4v - appear to be have been added in the seventeenth century by the owner who records that the volume came to him from Husum on 26 July 1603 with the remark that this happened 'after salvation had been reestablished', an emphatic form of writing 'Anno domini' with possible overtones of the Reformation as part of salvation history: *Liber Johannes KLincheri F. ex Donatione Jonas Folquardi, Ciuis Husenses. Anno restauratae salutis 1603 postridie D. Jacobi.*

The proverbs are in both German and Latin. The text on A4r, code-switching between Latin and German, starts in the middle of a sentence, arguing that God will come to the rescue: *Sed Violenter oppressus, iniuriæ poculum bibe.* || *Violenter opprimor, Sed ille dixit mihi, & etiam faciet* || *Quia nomen eius I.N.R.I.* || *Oderunt me gratis.* || *Tantum propter Veritatem* || *Veritas odium parit. Sed* || *Deus adhuc Iudex in terra est.* || *Quaerat hic deus, Videat & iudicat.* || *In monte Videbit Deus.* || *Tandem bona Causa triumphat.* || *Deus Viuens, Deus Videns.* || *Facit iudicium iniuriam patientibus.* || *Suo tempore liberat.* || *Got richt, wan nemandt sprichtt. Ergo,* || *Mein Hulff vnd Ratt, Trost, Zuuersichtt* || *Bistu allein Herr Jhesu Christ.* This is continued on the right-hand side: *Spes mea Christus.* || *Fons Vitae Christus.* || *Iudica Dominus nocen*||*tes me. Psal 34* || *Justis es Domine. Et ius-*||*ta iudicia tua.* || *Ecce infirmor hic.* The theme of God as judge and helper of the oppressed runs through the text, together with a firm trust in Christ: the letters 'INRI' stand out from the entry as does the underlined statement that 'all of this is because of Truth'.

The empty last page shows a similar mix of languages and sources, with four Bible quotations on praying for release from oppression (Is 38: 14) and rejoicing in adversity (2 Cor 7: 13) and two short Psalm statements about God as judge (Ps 43: 22 and Ps 5: 11). The German rhyming couplets thrown in are taken from different dialect areas: before the quotation from Corinthians there is the assurance in High German that no evil man will last before God (*Der Bösen Raeth wirt balde vorghan / Vor Got kein Böser mach besthann*), while the Psalm statements are introduced with a Low German verse about longing to be somewhere else (*Ick bin nicht, dar ik bin,* || *Dar ick nicht bin, dar is min sin*). And in the middle of it all is a proverb that is also used by Martin Luther about suffering first, enjoying glory later: *Priores passiones Posteriores glorias* (WA 44, 199, 17).

These verses and proverbs are neither original texts nor direct quotations from trusted authorities, but rather *ad hoc* compilations of proverbs, quotations, and popular sentiment; they were just accumulated from memory in much the same way that Luther kept a notebook for sayings,[140] rather than being an extract from a collection such as the popular *Adagia* edited by Erasmus. How the same phrases can be clustered together in different ways is apparent on the title page where originally there were only two lines of text:

---

[140] Notebook Oxford, Bodleian Library MS Add. A. 92, cf. the blog post by Alexander Peplow from 28 October 2017 on teachingthecodex.com.

a proverb which reinforces the notion of being made invisible by the powers that be (*Inuisus modo immerito*) and the German saying also found on A4r that God is judge even if there is nobody who is able to make a formal accusation: *Got richt, wan niemand spricht.*[141] When Johannes Klinker added his ownership entry, he also underlined both statements and added to the first another line with the word 'invisible' which linked to the theme of oppression: *Calcat jacentem Vulgus, inuisum opprimet*, and repeated the statement which had been underlined on A4r that all this is about truth. Together with his emphasis that the date follows the Reformation, this reveals a strong Protestant identity nearly a century after the pamphlet was first printed and a continuing acknowledgement of the liberating power of the text.

There are three further names given on the title page: in the right-hand bottom corner *Jacobus Laurentius* is in a hand which seems to predate Klinker; in the top right-hand corner *F. Mollers* is in a somewhat later hand; clearly an even later entry is *Petri 1719*, written with a flourish next to the title. Though it proved impossible to identify any of the owners, a clear pattern of use emerges: this is a string of Protestant readers proud of Reformation heritage and eager to associate themselves with the text by adding their name and mark to it. In a way, this has remained the case until the 20th century, as the acquisition history below shows.

Taken together, the Oxford copies of the *Sermon* thus allow an insight into Reformation as a process: how the pamphlet war shaped the development of print production, how it defined standards for presenting vernacular theological texts, and how the appeal of short, powerful texts in the vernacular secured the success of the movement.

---

[141] Wander, Deutsches Sprichwörter-Lexikon 2, 42 s.v. Gott, no. 963.

2.2 Acquisition

Christina Ostermann

The two versions of Luther's *Sermon on Indulgences and Grace* in the Taylor Institution reflect not only Reformation history, but also the physical history of the copies themselves. Both items show various additions which clearly mark them out as historical objects: ownership marks, stamps, and pencil notes all inform our understanding of the development of the library as a teaching collection and the role of its Reformation pamphlets as teaching materials.

A Duplicate from Heidelberg: Arch. 8° G. 1518 (5)

For both pamphlets, the first trace of the Taylorian can be found on the upper pastedown. In the case of Arch. 8° G. 1518 (5), an early *Ex libris* of the Taylor Institution Library has been added (ill. 17). It features the coats of arms both of the University of Oxford and of Sir Robert Taylor, the eponymous founder of the Institution. Underneath, a date added in pencil points to the year when the pamphlet entered the library: '1878'. This edition of the *Sermon von Ablass und Gnade* was therefore part of the first major acquisition drive of the library, which had only opened its doors in 1849.[142] In the early years of the Taylorian, roughly £250 a year was spent on new books while the bills for the newly constructed building still had to be paid. In 1874, however, Max Müller, deputy Taylorian Professor of Modern

[142] John Macray, the Taylorian's first librarian, had been in post from as early as 1847. The first books were purchased in 1848, one year before the library officially opened. Cf. Jill Hughes, Taylor Institution Library, in: Handbuch deutscher historischer Buchbestände in Europa. Vol. 10: A guide to the collections printed in German-speaking countries before 1901 (or in German elsewhere) held by libraries in Great Britain and Ireland, ed. by Graham Jefcoate, William A. Kelly and Karen Kloth. Hildesheim 2000, 309–18, here: 310.

European Languages from 1850 and Oxford's first Professor of Comparative Philology from 1860, persuaded the Curators to allocate an extra sum of £500 to allow the library to purchase items related to one of his main research areas, the history of language and literature. Müller's successful request led to the acquisition of both incunables and Reformation pamphlets in the 1870s and 1880s.[143] The Basel edition of the *Sermon* was among these very first pamphlets that came to Oxford at Müller's suggestion.

A search through the Taylorian's archives reveals that Arch. 8° G. 1518 (5) arrived at the library on 2 December 1878 as one of 139 Lutheran pamphlets bought from London bookseller David Nutt for a total price of £25.[144] On the title, the number '25' is still visible and could refer to this sum. It is, however, more likely that it corresponds to the number given to this pamphlet by Nutt. In his invoice (ill. 13), he lists 139 non-consecutive numbers as abbreviations for the 139 pamphlets sold. Arch. 8° G. 1530 (9), Luther's *Sendbrief vom Dolmetschen* was likewise acquired from Nutt in 1878 and features the number '22' on A1r. In his invoice, Nutt also states that all of these pamphlets were duplicates from Heidelberg University Library. Our pamphlet still shows a blue stamp on A1v (cf. facsimile F4) and A4r (F14) that reads *DVPLVM BIBLIOTH. HEIDELBERG.*

As soon as the pamphlet entered the library, a place for it had to be found. To identify its exact location(s), the upper pastedown again proves useful (ill. 17). It shows not only the current shelfmark Arch. 8° G. 1518 (5), but also two older ones, both crossed out: 92 b 16 and Arch II b 5.[145] This change in shelfmark indicates a change of location

[143] Cf. Hughes 2000, 310–11.

[144] David Nutt's invoice from 29 November 1878 can be found in the Taylorian Archives. Cf. Oxford University Archives, TL 2/14/4: Vouchers received from suppliers for payments made, with some cleared cheques 1877–82.

[145] The earliest shelfmark, 92 b 16, is also visible on the bottom of A1r (facsimile F2), again written in pencil.

in the library. When the pamphlet first came to the Taylorian, it was put in the 92nd bookcase, which can still be found on the upper gallery in the main reading room. It was placed on the second shelf from the top, shelf 'b', and was the sixteenth volume along. In the 20th century, the pamphlet then became part of the 'Arch' – short for 'Archives' – collection and was moved from this open bookcase to the second of five antique church vestry cupboards which were also located in the upper gallery. Here, it was again placed on the second shelf ('b'), fifth along. Nowadays, the pamphlet is even more safely stowed: like all 'Arch' material, it is kept in the Taylorian's strongroom.

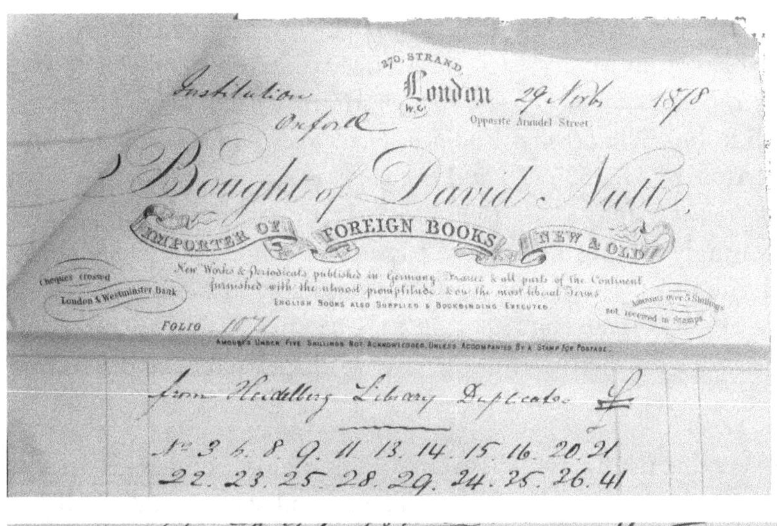

Institution Oxford

270, Strand, London W.C. 29 Nov 1878
Opposite Arundel Street

Bought of David Nutt,
Importer of Foreign Books New & Old

New Works & Periodicals published in Germany, France & all parts of the Continent furnished with the utmost promptitude & on the most liberal Terms
English Books also Supplied & Bookbinding Executed

Cheques crossed London & Westminster Bank

Amounts over 5 Shillings not received in Stamps

Folio 1671

Amounts Under Five Shillings Not Acknowledged, Unless Accompanied By A Stamp For Postage.

from Heidelberg Library Duplicates £

No 3. 6. 8. 9. 11. 13. 14. 15. 16. 20. 21
22. 23. 25. 28. 29. 24. 35. 36. 41

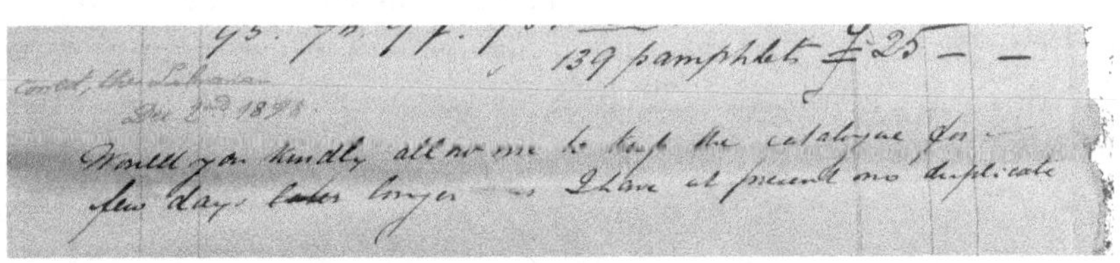

139 pamphlets £25 — —

Correct, the Librarian
Dec 2nd 1878

Would you kindly allow me to keep the catalogue for a few days longer — I have at present no duplicate

Ill. 13: Invoice for Reformation pamphlets from David Nutt 29 Nov 1878
and the Librarian's note that the sums are correct
Oxford University Archives, TL 2/14/4

An Annotated Rarity: Arch. 8° G. 1518 (6)

The second copy of the *Sermon von Ablass und Gnade* came to the Taylorian nearly fifty years after the first. The *Ex libris* we find on the upper pastedown features a later coat of arms (cf. illustrations 17/18 of both *Ex libris* on p. lxxviii), and a stamp on A4v gives the exact date: 11 April 1927. On this day, the Taylorian's cashbook lists a payment of £2.2s.0d (= £2.10) to London bookseller Myers.[146] For this purchase, the library used money available via the Finch fund, a sum bequeathed to the Bodleian, Ashmolean, and Taylorian by Oxford-educated antiquarian Robert Finch (1783–1830) to share and spend on the acquisition of books.

Two months earlier, the library had already acquired three other pamphlets from Myers, each for a price of £1.10s.0d (= £1.50): *Eyn vnterrichtunge, wie sich die Christen yn Mosen sollen schicken* (Arch. 8° G. 1526 (8)), *Ein Sermon Von dem Heubtman zu Capernaum, Matth. viij.* (Arch. 8° G. 1535 (7)) and *Ein einfeltige weise zu Beten, fur einen guten freund* (Arch. 8° G. 1535 (2)).[147] It is clear that the library was increasingly willing and able to pay up for single pamphlets – even for a title already in its holdings. What arguably makes this particular copy of the *Sermon von Ablass und Gnade* special are the numerous annotations on the title and the last two pages which add a second historical layer (cf. above).

The fact that the library was aware of this double purchase is evident in the location of the pamphlets. The invalid shelfmark Arch II b 6 testifies to the fact that the second *Sermon* was placed right next to the first one: in the second church vestry cupboard in the upper gallery, on the second shelf, the sixth volume along.

---

[146] For Myers' invoice cf. Oxford University Archives, TL 3/2/8: New additions to the library (1922–34).

[147] A snippet of Myers' auction catalogue which lists all three pamphlets bought in February 1927 can still be found in Arch. 8° G. 1526 (8).

3. How to Read the *Sermon*

Henrike Lähnemann

A sermon is a piece of prose meant to be performed: read out loud, performed with gestures, drawing the audience in. This holds true even for the text published here, which is likely to be a shortened and recast version of the original spoken sermon. When we read out and recorded the *Sendbrief vom Dolmetschen* to go with the edition of that work in this series of Luther pamphlets, we were struck by how the rhetorical indicators in the text served as cues for performance and brought the text to life.

The following short guide is therefore meant to provide pointers to oral delivery, to allow readers to lift the text off the page and understand the different system of punctuation, spelling, and structuring used for its printed representation. This has since been added to – much of the underlining done by an early reader in the Leipzig copy may have been designed to facilitate delivery, e.g. in §9: *Aber wir haben mehr freyheyt czuuorachten (got lob) sulchs vnnd des gleychen plauderey/ dañ sie haben czu ertichten / dañ alle peyn /ya alls was gott auff legt/ ist besserlich vnd tzu treglich den Christen.*

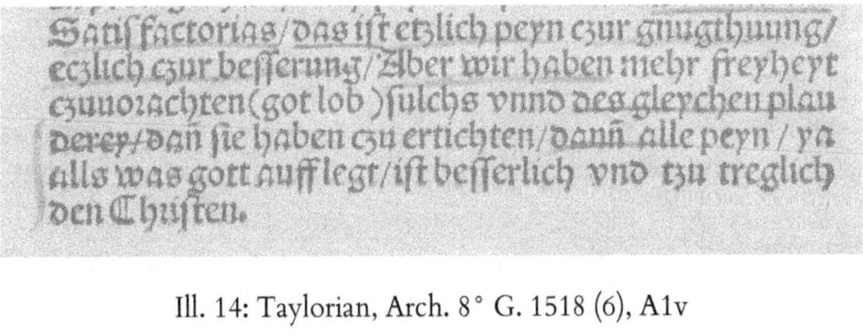
Satiſfactorias/das iſt etzlich peyn czur gnugthuung/ etzlich czur beſſerung/Aber wir haben mehr freyheyt czuuorachten(got lob)ſulchs vnnd des gleychen plau derey/dañ ſie haben czu ertichten/dañ alle peyn / ya alls was gott auff legt/iſt beſſerlich vnd tzu treglich den Chriſten.

Ill. 14: Taylorian, Arch. 8° G. 1518 (6), A1v

1. Punctuation
   Early modern editions use full stops, brackets, question marks, and virgules ('/') primarily to help users punctuate their speech

rather than as grammatical markers. It is useful to think of the whole *Sermon* as a recitative and the punctuation as musical notation, as in the example above where the interjection 'thank God' is marked in parentheses, indicating an interruption in the flow of argument to be stressed in speech to capture the audience's attention.[148]

. The point is used both for full stops at the end of sentences and for other strong interruptions of the speech flow where in modern punctuation a semicolon, a colon, or even just a comma would be used, as in §6 *Jtem also hatt er selbs all die absoluirt. Maria Magda. den gichtpruchtigē. Die eebrecherynne &c.* With modern punctuation this would read *Item, also hatt er selbs all die absolviert: Maria Magdalena, den Gichtprüchtigen, die Ehebrecherinne etc.*

/ The virgula (forward slash) is the main means of structuring sentences, standing for the modern comma and functioning like a musical caesura. It helps to create a rhythmical structure, particularly noticeable in the last paragraph of the *Sermon* where Luther builds the argument up to a crescendo with a dramatic sequence of parallel syntactic units. He claims not to care for *eczlich finster gehyrne / die die Biblien nie gerochē / die Christenlichē lerer nie geleszē* [/] *yhr eigen lerer nie vorstanden / sundern in yhren lochereten vnd czurissen opinien vill nah vorwesen.* If we were to mark up the translation accordingly, it would run: *certain dark minds / who have never been within smelling distance of the Bible / never read the Christian teachers / never understood their own teachers / but under their tattered threadbare opinions are all but wasting away.* In the Leipzig print, no virgule is needed after *geleszē* because a line break acts as the equivalent structural marker. This shows how punctuation is adapted to the physical copy and, like

148 Henrike Lähnemann and Michael Rupp, Parenthese, in: Historisches Wörterbuch der Rhetorik 6 (2003), cols 573–76.

spelling, reflects the production of the text by the printer rather than exactly reproducing a predefined text.

2. Abbreviations
   Early printing took over from manuscripts some handy ways to save space. The main abbreviation mark is a dash '‾' over a character. Most frequently it is a nasal bar to replace a following *-n*, as in the Leipzig edition (L) §3: *Beeten / vastē / almuszē* which in the Basel (B) version reads *Baͤtten / vasten / almůsen*, but it also can replace *-m*, as in B §19 *Zů dē neünzehenden* (the previous paragraph has the full form: *Zů dem achtzehenden*). There are also a number of established abbreviations for frequent words, mainly 'dz' = *das* (only in B), 'vñ' = *und*, and 'd'' = *der*. Other abbreviations are used for references such as 'p̄s' (L) or 'Psal.' (B) = *Psalm*. Twice in L, points used for punctuation double up as abbreviation marks (*Magda.* for *Magdalena* and *Sentē.* for *Sententiarum*). Capital 'S' as a title for saints is enclosed between two points, which function as space marker for the extreme abbreviation, and has to be resolved in accordance with whether the name or title is referred to in Latin or German. Thus *.S. Petri* (§15) is based on the Latin name of the apostle *Petrus* and needs to be resolved with a matching Latin case ending as *Sancti Petri*, while he is called by his German name *Peter* in the next paragraph; *.S. Peters* (§16) therefore reads either as *Sankt* or *Sant Peters* – both German forms come up in full in the same paragraph. The first paragraph in L reads: *Czum Ersten solt yr wissen / das eczlich new lerer / als Magister Sentē .S. Thomas vñ yhre folger gebē d' pusz drey teyl.* With modern spelling and punctuation, this would run as *Zum ersten sollt ihr wissen, dass ezlich neu Lehrer, als Magister Sententiarum Sanctus* (or *San(c)t* since the name Thomas is identical in Latin and German) *Thomas und ihre Folger, geben der Puß* (= Buße) *drei Teil.*

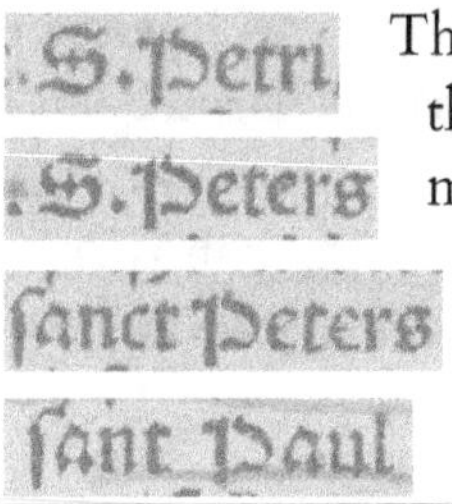

Ill. 15: Forms of Saint in L, Arch. 8° G. 1518 (6), A3r/v

3. *u/v/w – i/j/y – v/f*, and different *s* and *r* forms
The Roman alphabet had only one symbol for *u* and *v* and one for *i* and *j*. *u/v/w* (double *u*) and *i/j* (long *i*)/*y* (double *i*) are therefore graphic variants, not distributed according to their function as vowels or consonants, e.g. *vnd* (und), *trewe* (Treue), *yhn* (ihn); *v/f* are both used for *f*, similarly to modern German. The two typographically different forms for *s* (*s* at the end, long *ſ* otherwise) and *r* (*ꝛ* mostly after *o*, sometimes after *b*, *d*, *h*, *p*, otherwise *r*) have not been distinguished.

Ill. 16: *voꝛfurt*
L §16, A3v

4. Umlaut and superscript *e* and *o*
The umlaut sound would in most cases have been in the same position as in modern German but there is no strict rule for writing it; the Leipzig print shows no diacritical mark at all and only keeps the Middle High German convention of writing the umlaut of *a* as *e*, e.g. §20 *lestern / vnuorhort vn̄ vnuberwundē* for *lästern, unverhört, und unüberwunden*. By contrast, the Basel print frequently uses umlaut dots for *ü*, e.g. in *fünf* and *sünde*, also occasionally after *e* (*neünzehen*), and makes an excessive use of superscript *e*: it not only serves for umlaut of long and short *a, o, u* (e.g. *lasz die faulen schlaͤfferigen ablasz loͤsen* for *laß die faulen Schläferigen Ablass lösen*) but is also used (unhistorically) for *e* as in *haͤrtzliche* for *herzliche*. The Basel printer is fairly consistent in the use of *ů*, i.e. superscript *o* over *u*, for the Middle High German *uo*. The same sentence in §14 thus reads in Leipzig *wollen kecklich vben in guten wercken* and in Basel *woͤlle kaͤcklich uͤben yn gůten werckē*. When reading the text out loud, readers should use umlauts where they would be in standard modern German, or enjoy the freedom to modify the vowel sounds to fit their own dialect (cf. 'Language and Style' §§8–9).

5. Double versus single consonants and *s/sz/ß, k/ck, z/cz/tz*
There is no consistency in writing single and double consonant such as *f/ff* or *n/nn* (except that the doubled spelling is avoided

at the beginning of words), and they can be pronounced alike (but see §3 of 'Language and Style' below). This also applies to the *s* forms. *ß* started out as a ligature of *ſ* and *ʒ* to indicate a double consonant and can be typeset as one character *ß* or as two distinct letters *sz*, e.g. *ablasz*, *ablaß* and *ablas*; *ck* is the spelling for double *k*; *cz/tz* is the spelling for *z*. A comparison between the two editions can be helpful: L *Funffczehenden* would have been pronounced like B *fünffzehenden*.

6. Use of *h* and *e* after vowels
   The use of *h* after a long preceding vowel is not consistent, e.g. *nehmen* and *nemen* are used interchangeably; *ee* indicates long *e* (*seele*). As for *ie/ye*, whether these were read as a diphthong or long *i* would have depended on the dialect of the reader. See §§2 and 9–10 of 'Language and Style' below.

7. Hyphenation, word division, and mergers
   Hyphens in the form of '=' are used frequently, but not consistently, to indicate the continuation of words across line breaks (*ge=||bewde* and *ge||weyset*). Split words have been linked in the transcription but the irregular use of spaces in-line such as *got lob* and *gottlob*, *czuuorachten* and *czu vben*, *inszfegfewr* and *ausz dē fegfewr* has not been normalized, even though it might just reflect the typesetter adapting to how much or little space was left in a line.

8. Capital letters
   Capital letters are used as in English to indicate the beginning of new sentences and for proper names but also for other words such as *Creucz*, Latin terms such as *Medicatiuas* and *Satisfactorias* for the two types of *peyn*, or the numbering of the paragraphs as in *Czum Sechsten*; these have not been normalized since they highlight key points in the text.

4. Language and Style

Howard Jones

This section summarizes the differences between the German of Luther's time and today's standard language, compares the language of the two printed pamphlets ('prints') in this edition, and discusses Luther's style. Further linguistic comments can be found in the notes to the transcriptions.

Phonology – general comments

We set out below the main phonological differences between the language of the *Sermon* and present-day standard German ('New High German' or 'NHG'), and we comment on the dialect features of the two prints reproduced in this volume.

The modern reader is struck by the inconsistency in the spelling of Early New High German (ENHG)[149] texts such as those in this edition. Some spelling variants represent the same sounds; these are discussed in 'How to Read the *Sermon*' above. The spelling variants dealt with in this section are those which reflect phonological variation, corresponding to language change at the time, dialect differences, or features of the spoken language.

The prints reproduced here were made in Leipzig and Basel (see chapter 2.1. 'Production' above), abbreviated here to 'L' and 'B' (or 'LB' if reference is made to both); numbered references are to points 1–20 of the *Sermon*. L is close in its spelling to the Wittenberg prints of the *Sermon*, and its dialect features are largely those associated with the East Central German area in which both Leipzig and Wittenberg

[149] Early New High German (ENHG) refers to the German language between 1350 and 1650, Middle High German (MHG) to 1050–1350, and Old High German to the period before 1050.

are situated. The spelling of B diverges from that of L in ways that are characteristic of the Low Alemannic dialect area where Basel is located. However, as is typical of ENHG texts, both L and B include spellings which are not primarily associated with their own dialect areas. The transcription of L is contained in this volume; that of B can be found on the website editions.mml.ox.ac.uk.

Phonology - Typical Early New High German features found in both prints

§1 *Omission of unstressed ‹e›*. The omission of ‹e› in the middle of a word (reflecting syncope) or at the end (apocope) is widespread, e.g. 'seins fleyschs' (L3), 'dritt' (L2), respectively. When the consonants either side of the unstressed vowel are the same or similar, one of them may also be lost (by 'haplology'), e.g. 'desz ablas' (L15; here the ending *-es* is omitted), 'gegrund' (L19; for 'gegrundet'), 'czurissen' (L20; for 'czurissenen'). Sometimes unstressed vowels are spelt in the prints which are omitted in the equivalent NHG word, e.g. 'geteylet' (L3; cf. NHG *geteilt*); at other times unstressed vowels are omitted in the prints which are spelt in NHG, e.g. 'gnugthuung' (L1; NHG *Genugtuung*).

§2 *Marking of long vowels*. Long vowels may be marked with a following ‹h› as in NHG, e.g. 'hynnehme' (L5), 'wohl' (B12). This is more widespread in L but inconsistent in both prints, e.g. hyn neme (L9), 'wol' (B12). Long [e:] is sometimes marked by doubling, e.g. 'seelen' (L18), 'seer' (L20).[150]

§3 *Variation in single and double consonants.* Within both prints there is inconsistency even in the spelling of the same words, e.g. 'kann/kan' (L8, 11), 'will/wil' (B7), 'ablasz/ablas' (L15). This variation

[150] The marking of vowels in open syllables as long which had been short in MHG, such as in 'hynnehme' (cf. MHG *neme* with short [ɛ]), is consistent with such vowels generally having been lengthened (in line with NHG) by Luther's time.

reflects the breakdown of the phonological distinction between single and double consonants which operated in MHG, so that as a rule consonants were now pronounced short however they were spelt. As in NHG, double consonants tend to follow short vowels (except for ‹ff› – see below). However, as the examples just cited show, single consonants follow short vowels as well, so that the NHG practice of indicating a long vowel in a stressed medial syllable with a following single consonant and a short vowel with a following double consonant is not observed.[151] Printers sometimes used double consonants to fill up short lines and justify the text (in L4 we even find 'dannn').

Both texts have (often unhistorical) double ‹ff› in all positions except syllable-initially, e.g. 'Funfften' (L5), 'vnuorworffeñ' (L6), 'bedarff' (L16). This may signify a more fortis articulation than in syllable-initial position, where ‹f›, ‹v›, or ‹u› occurs, e.g. fleyschs (L3), 'vastē' (L3), 'vnuolkōmen' (L14).

§4 *The spellings ‹dt› and ‹th›*. The digraph ‹dt› often appears in syllable-final position where ‹d› would occur in NHG, e.g. 'todtsund' (L11), 'yemādt' (L13), 'nyemandt' (L16). The ‹dt› spelling is a compromise between the phonetic MHG spelling ‹t›, which reflects final devoicing, and the NHG spelling, which uses ‹d› consistently in a word if the sound is voiced in medial position (e.g. *niemandem*) and devoiced finally (*niemand*).[152]

The spelling ‹th› instead of NHG ‹t›, e.g. 'thun' (L4) reflects a learned practice associated with Humanism, possibly originating with

[151] We do not find consonant doubling used to make the graphemic distinction between *dass* and *das* as we do in NHG, e.g. 'das (eczlich)' (= NHG *dass*) and 'das (yczt)' (= NHG *das*) in L1.

[152] The spelling ‹gk› in 'Wittenbergk' in the title of both prints represents a similar compromise.

German words modelled on Greek or Latin cognates in θ or *th*, e.g. *thier* on Greek θήρ ‘wild animal’, or names such as *Thomas*.

§5 *Variation in final ‹t›*. There is an unhistorical final ‹t› in ‘den nocht’ (L9), possibly added to reproduce a sound that was thought by listeners to occur at the end of certain words.[153] Further examples are ‘yczt’ (L1) (cf. MHG *iez(e)*) and ‘selbst’ (L18), although in all other instances of the latter in both prints the historical ‘selbs’ occurs (e.g. LB6). Note that final ‹t› is omitted in ‘begreyff/begreiff’ (LB3) and ‘nich’ (L18).

§6 *The spellings ‹mpt› and ‹umb›*. In spellings such as ‘nympt’ (L2), ‘kumpt’ (L16), and ‘alsampt’ (L19), the [p] sound is unhistorical. It is a so-called ‘epenthetic glide consonant’, meaning that it has been inserted to bridge the articulatory gap between the sounds either side. Thus, like [m], [p] is bilabial, and like [t] it is a voiceless plosive, so it shares features with its immediate neighbours and eases articulation. By contrast, the [b] represented in ‘darumb’ (e.g. L14) is historical (cf. MHG *dar umbe*).

§7 *Contractions*. Both prints show contractions between words: ‘wiltu’, ‘magstu’, ‘saltu’, ‘halts’ (all from LB16), no doubt in imitation of spoken German.

Phonology – Differences between the prints

§8 *Umlaut*. In both prints ‹e› is used for NHG ‹ä›, e.g. ‘Nemlich’ (LB1), ‘vnsche̲czlicher’ (LB13). Otherwise umlaut is unmarked in L; this is typical of Central German texts of this period and does not point to non-umlauted pronunciation.[154] In B, ‹ʊͤ› stands for NHG

[153] See Hermann Paul, Mittelhochdeutsche Grammatik, Tübingen [25]2007, 140; and Charles V. J. Russ, Studies in Historical German Phonology. A Phonological Comparison of MHG and NHG with Reference to Modern Dialects, Bern/Frankfurt am Main 1982, 38–43.

[154] See also ‘erleubt’ and footnote (L17).

‹ö›, e.g. 'hoͤren' (B3), 'moͤchten' (B4), and ‹ü› occurs as in NHG, e.g. 'für' (B4), 'sünde' (B5). Note that the symbol ‹aͤ› in B is a spelling variant for ‹e› found particularly for a long vowel or before ‹r›, e.g. 'laͤsen', 'waͤrck' (both B3). On ‹uͤ›, see §9.

§9 *Monophthongization of MHG [uo], [üe], [ie].* In NHG these diphthongs have been monophthongized to [u:], [ü:], [i:], respectively. As is typical of ENHG texts from the Central German dialect area, this process is reflected in L, e.g. 'czuthun' (L4) for MHG *zuo tuon*, and 'vben' (L6) for MHG *üeben*. It is not possible to tell for certain whether ‹ie› represents a monophthong because this would be the spelling for the old diphthong as well. However, the fact that, in L, this spelling is used for the monophthong [i:] even when it is not the reflex of [ie] is consistent with its representing a monophthong throughout this print, e.g. 'vielē' (L5), 'syeben' (L11) – in these cases [i:] comes from the lengthening of [i] in open syllables, not from monophthongization.

In B, the diphthongal spellings ‹ů› and ‹uͤ› are typical of Alemannic texts of the time, reflecting the lack of monophthongization in this dialect area, e.g. 'zů thůn' (B4) and 'uͤben' (B6). As with L, it is not possible to tell for certain whether ‹ie› represents the old diphthong [ie] or its monophthongal reflex [i:]. However, unlike L, B uses the spelling ‹ie› only for what had been diphthongs in MHG (e.g. 'niemandt' B8, 'lieber' B9) and never for a long [i:] resulting from lengthening (e.g. 'vylen' B5, 'syben' B11). This is consistent with the spelling ‹ie› representing a diphthong, which would be in keeping with the diphthongal spellings ‹ů› and ‹uͤ›.

§10 *Diphthongization of MHG [u:], [ü:] (=‹iu›), [i:].* In NHG these monophthongs have been diphthongized to [au], [oi], and [ai], respectively. As is typical of ENHG texts from the Central German dialect area, this process is seen in L, e.g. 'auff' (L6) (MHG *ûf*), 'newen' (L9) and 'euch' (L16) (MHG *niuwen, iuch*), and 'deynē/dein' (L16) (MHG *dîn*).

For the most part, B has diphthongal spellings too, e.g. 'auff' (B6), 'newen' (B9) and 'eüch' (B16), 'dein' (B16). However, this does not mirror the pronunciation in the Low Alemannic dialect area around Basel, where diphthongization did not, in general, take place. There are counter-examples to these diphthongal spellings, however, e.g. 'vff' (B16), 'luter' (B15), 'nündē' (B9), 'verzyhet' (B13; cf. L13 'vorczeyhet' where the diphthong is spelt).[155]

§11 *Vowel rounding*. B shows rounding of [i] to [ü] in 'würckest' (B18), 'gehürne' (B20), and 'wüstē' (B20) (cf. 'wirckest', 'gehyrne', and 'wisten' in L) and rounding of [e] to [ö] in 'zwoͤlfften' (B12) (cf. 'czwelfftē' in L). The rounded forms are associated with the Alemannic dialect area. Note that NHG has adopted some rounded forms but not others.

§12 *Variation between ‹a› and ‹o› in certain words*. L tends to show the ‹a› spelling and B the ‹o› spelling in 'ader/oder' (e.g. LB15), 'ab/ob' (e.g. LB5), 'sall/soll' (e.g. LB11). The ‹a› spellings are associated particularly with the East Central German dialect area. However, there are some counter-examples in each print, e.g. 'soll' (L14), 'ader' (B12). The ‹o› spellings become more common in Luther's later writings.

§13 *Variation between the prefix 'vor-' and 'ver-'*. L usually has the typical Central German prefix *vor-* where B has the typical Upper German prefix *ver-*, e.g. 'vorlassen/verlassen' (LB9) and 'vorfurt/verfuͤrt' (LB16). However, B also has a few instances of *vor-*, e.g. 'vorspricht' (B7).

---

[155] For details on the geographical extent of diphthongization, see Oskar Reichmann, Klaus-Peter Wegera (eds), Frühneuhochdeutsche Grammatik, Tübingen 1993, 64–67; and Peter Wiesinger, Phonetisch-phonologische Untersuchungen zur Vokalentwicklung in den deutschen Dialekten. 1: Die Langvokale im Hochdeutschen, Berlin 1970, 86–95, 183–91.

§14 *Variation between long vowel and diphthong in words beginning ‹je› in NHG*. The variation in spelling in, e.g. 'yczt' (L1) vs 'jetzund' (B1) and 'yglich' (L11) vs 'jegliche' (B11), points to a characteristic dialect difference between the long vowel [i:] in Central German and the diphthong [ie] in Upper German. However, the contrast shows up only in certain words: in 'yemand' (L10) and 'yederman' (L11), L, like B, reflects a diphthongal pronunciation (and B has an exceptional 'jtzet' in B11). Note that, in NHG, ‹je› represents [jɛ], a semi-vowel followed by a vowel, which is different from both [i:] and [ie].

§15 *Other dialect features*. See notes to 'pusz' (L1), 'erbeiten' (L3), 'gottis' (L7), 'sulchs' (L9), 'brengen' (L10), 'erleubt' (L17), 'flaischs' (B3), 'stot' (B7), and 'syen' (B10).

Morphology

Both prints have examples of MHG inflections which have not survived into NHG.

§16 *Nouns*. There are some feminine nouns with weak MHG endings (i.e. -(*e*)*n* in all cases, singular and plural, except for the nominative singular in -(*e*)), e.g. dative singular 'der seelē' (L3), 'der ruthen' (L7), and accusative singular 'die Biblien' (L20). Other feminine nouns decline with strong MHG endings (i.e. -(*e*) in all cases except for the dative and (sometimes) genitive plural in -(*e*)*n*), e.g. '(disze) peyne' (nominative singular; L7), '(zweyerley) peyne' (accusative plural; L9). There are also strong neuter nouns with uninflected nominative/accusative plural forms as in MHG, e.g. 'gute werck' (L5).

As for strong adjectives, the nominative singular of all genders and the accusative neuter and feminine singular had alternative uninflected forms in ENHG (as in MHG); we see this, for example, in 'hart lager' (L3) and 'hart ligē' (B3) where the adjective would be 'hartes' in NHG.

§17 *Verbs*. In 'fund' (LB16; = *fünde*), we have the MHG form of the preterite subjunctive of *finden*; this has become *fände* in NHG, where all forms of the preterite now show *a* (indicative) or *ä* (subjunctive) by analogy with the historical indicative preterite singular *fand*. Among weak verb forms we find 'gedaucht' (LB6) (the past participle of *dünken*), which is the reflex of the MHG *gedûht* showing diphthongization of [u:] to [au]; see §10. However, there is also the form 'gedunckten/gedūckten' in LB8, which shows levelling to the infinitive/present.[156]

The main morphological contrasts between the prints are that L has the typically Central German 'sein' as the third-person plural present indicative of the verb 'to be' where B has the typical Upper German 'sind', e.g. 'seyn/sind' (LB11),[157] and B has the typically Alemannic first- and second-person plural ending *-ent* (or here *-end* with [t] voiced to [d] by assimilation with [n]) in 'sͤollend (jr)' and 'wellēd (wir)' (B1).

§18 *Latin inflections*. A common feature of ENHG religious texts is the Latin inflection of Latin words, as seen, for example, in 'Christi' (L6), 'doctores' (L6), 'doctorem' (title B), 'Medicatiuas' (L9), 'Petri' (L15), and 'scholasticos' (L19).

Lexis

§19 The terms around which the argument in the *Sermon* revolves are (with the translations used in this edition) 'ablasz' 'indulgence', 'gnad' 'grace', 'pusz/bůsz' 'penance', 'peycht/beycht' 'confession', 'peyn' 'punishment', and 'gnugthuung' 'satisfaction'. See 'Theological and Historical Background'.

---

[156] Note that the (archaic) NHG forms of the preterite and past participle *deuchte/gedeucht* are based on the MHG preterite subjunctive form *diuhte* (with diphthongization of [ü:] to [oi]; see §10).

[157] L has one example of 'sind' in 19.

Some words in the *Sermon* have different meanings from those of their reflexes in NHG or have dropped out of use. The differences are made clear in the translation or the notes to the transcriptions, but those which occur frequently in the text are listed below:

- *als* can mean 'as' corresponding to NHG *wie*, e.g. 'als wachen … , L3;
- *dann* can mean 'than' corresponding to NHG *als*, e.g. 'dan̄ alleyne gottis', L7;
- *ob* can mean 'if' or 'even if', corresponding to NHG (*auch*) *wenn*, e.g. 'ob die Christenliche kirch … ', L9;
- *so* can serve as a conjunction meaning 'if/when', e.g. 'szo du wilt' 'if you wish', L16;
- *vor* in L can mean NHG *für*, e.g. 'vor ein yglich todtsund' 'for each mortal sin', L11 (cf. 'für ein jegliche totsünd' in B11);
- *wol* tends to mean 'very' or 'indeed' rather than 'probably' as in NHG, e.g. 'Vn̄d mocht woll gerne … ' 'And I would very much like … ', L6.

The two prints sometimes show different choices from variant forms, e.g. 'schrifft/geschryfft' (LB1), 'gebewde/gebew' (LB15), 'schmuck/geschmuck' (LB16); other lexical differences between the prints are mentioned in the notes to the transcriptions.

Syntax

§20 *Use of the subjunctive.* The subjunctive is used more widely in the *Sermon* than it would be in NHG. For example, it is found in subordinate clauses which depend on another clause which is negative or doubtful, as in the following cases:

> Jst bey vielē gewest eyn groſʒe vn̄ noch vnbeschloszene opiny / Ab der ablas auch etwas mehr <u>hynnehme</u> (L5)

Das sag ich / das mā ausz keyner schrifft bewerenn kañ / das gottlich gerechtigkeyt etwas peyn adder gnugthuung begere adder fordere (L6)

In NHG the equivalents of the underlined verbs would be in the indicative.

The subjunctive is also found after commands or implicit commands where NHG would have the indicative, e.g.

sall mā achtē / das nicht mehr auffgelegt werde dañ yederman wol tragē kan (L11)

and in concessive clauses, e.g.

Wann gleych ('even if') die pusz ym geystlichē recht geseczt / iczt noch ginge (L11)

Luther makes widespread use of subordinate clauses without conjunctions to introduce indirect discourse, e.g.

Czum andernñ sagen sie / der ablasz nympt nycht hynn das erst adder ander teyll (L2)

Ja er will sie nit lassen / sūder vorspricht / er woll sie aufflegē (L7)

The verb in the subordinate clause may be in the indicative or subjunctive, as these two examples show, respectively. The use of such 'unintroduced' subordinate clauses, with either mood, is also found in NHG, with the indicative associated particularly with colloquial usage. In ENHG such constructions are widespread even in official texts, and do not necessarily indicate a low register.[158]

[158] For an example in a royal declaration, see Wladimir Admoni, Die Entwicklung des Ganzsatzes und seines Wortbestandes in der deutschen Literatursprache bis zum Ende des 18. Jahrhunderts, in: Günther Feudel (ed.), Studien zur Geschichte der deutschen Sprache, Berlin 1972, 263–64.

§21 *Genitive phrases.* There are examples in the *Sermon* of a genitive noun or phrase placed before the noun on which it depends, rather than after (as would be expected in NHG), e.g. 'czu der Christenheyt schmach' (L10), 'von der dinger czall' (L17). The latter of these is also an example of a 'partitive genitive', a phrase which denotes part of what is mentioned in the genitive. There are a number of such constructions in the *Sermon*, some of which would have to be rephrased in NHG. For example, 'vill gutter werck' (L16) literally 'much of good works' corresponds to NHG 'viele gute Werke'.

§22 *Word order in verb phrases.* In the great majority of (i) main clauses in which there is more than one verbal element and (ii) subordinate clauses, there is a full verbal bracket with no 'Nachfeld', that is, with none of the clause occurring after the right-hand part of the bracket. Here is an example in which there are two co-ordinated main clauses, each with a full verbal bracket:

> darumb soll man nit wider das ablas redenn / man sall aber auch nyemand darczu reden (L14)

In the following subordinate clause (also quoted above), there is again a full verbal bracket, formed this time of the conjunction 'Wann gleych' (= NHG *wenngleich*) and the finite verb 'ginge':

> Wann gleych die pusz ym geystlichē recht geseczt / iczt noch ginge … (L11)

However, there are counter-examples, as in the following main clause and subordinate clause, respectively ('Nachfeld' underlined):

> die gnugthuung wirt weyter geteylet in drey teil (L3)

> … die sich nit wollen kecklich vben in guten wercken (L14)

The order of verbal elements at the end of a subordinate clause is generally in line with the prevailing order in NHG, that is, with the finite verb in final position,[159] e.g. 'wer das anders bewerē soll' (L6), but there are exceptions, such as, 'Szo ('if') seyn kinder werden sundigen … ' (L7), where the NHG order would be 'sundigen werden'.

In modern German the creation of a 'Nachfeld' and the placing of the non-finite verb element after the finite element in a subordinate clause are associated with colloquial or dialectal usage. However, it is unlikely that either practice was associated particularly with spoken, as opposed to written, German at the time Luther was writing the *Sermon*. Word order in subordinate clauses has been shown to reflect a mix of factors at the time, including the type and register of text, the role and status of the writer, the need to disambiguate subordinate clauses from main clauses, and, in translated texts, the word order of the original.[160] On 'unintroduced' subordinate clauses, see §20.

Style

In many respects the style of the *Sermon* is in line with German prose style at the time and is not peculiar to Luther. For any vernacular writing of the period we must allow for the linguistic differences between ENHG and NHG outlined above and for the fact that, in the intervening period, German has become standardized in spelling and grammar. German has also, since Luther's time, developed an abstract vocabulary that was not available at that time, Latin being the medium for most academic discourse, so that even on serious

---

[159] The main exception to this order in NHG is in subordinate clauses in which there are two infinitives, one of which is the infinitive of a modal verb serving as a participle, e.g. … *weil er den Brief hätte schreiben sollen*.

[160] For summaries of the literature, including references to studies on Luther's word order, see Anne Betten, Grundzüge der Prosasyntax. Stilprägende Entwicklungen vom Althochdeutschen zum Neuhochdeutschen, Tübingen 1987, 127–37; and Jürg Fleischer and Oliver Schallert, Historische Syntax des Deutschen. Eine Einführung, Tübingen 2011, 159–73.

topics the lexis of the vernacular may appear strikingly concrete to the modern reader.

Two important precedents in Luther's time for serious German prose writing were chancery (that is, legal and administrative) documents and the sermons of earlier preachers. The contrast between the style of the *Sermon* and that of chancery documents betrays their different purposes. Chancery documents, whose content was often complex and legalistic, include lengthy subordinate clauses, often nested in each other down to several levels, and placed at the beginning of the sentence, during which the addressee has to wait for the arrival of the main clause (typically a declaration or command). Word order in subordinate clauses in chancery documents is largely in line with NHG practice, that is, with the finite verb at the end.[161] In the *Sermon*, by contrast, there is rarely more than one level of subordination, the subordinate clause typically follows the main clause, and word order in such clauses can be variable, as shown in §22 above.

Vernacular sermons in German date back to the High Middle Ages, with Berthold von Regensburg (c. 1210–72), Meister Eckhart (c. 1260–1328), and Johannes Tauler (1300–61) the best known exponents in Luther's time. Luther was certainly familiar with the works of Tauler as well as with an anonymous work of mysticism which has come to be called *Theologia Deutsch*, which Luther admired for its spare, unadorned language.[162] Indeed, some of the stylistic aspects of the *Sermon* are shared with the sermons of his forerunners and the *Theologia Deutsch*: the simple syntax, largely comprising short co-ordinated main clauses (e.g. 3), the use of the first and second person for preacher and addressee (e.g. 16), references to 'man' (e.g. 14) and the inclusive 'wir' for generalizations

---

[161] For examples, see Admoni, Die Entwicklung des Ganzsatzes.

[162] See Erwin Arndt and Gisela Brandt, Luther und die deutsche Sprache, Leipzig 1983, 14.

(e.g. 4), and questions and answers to help make points through imaginary dialogue (e.g. 16).

However, Luther's prose style stands out from that of his predecessors. The following features, illustrated in the *Sermon*, are considered characteristic of his German writing.

§23 *Directness.* A good example in the *Sermon* is in the exposition in 1–5, and particularly in 3 where Luther lists the three components of satisfaction before defining each in turn, all in short, paratactic sentences (similar to bullet-points today). However, directness is not synonymous with simplicity: in 8 he draws a stark logical conclusion from the preceding points but in a dense, grammatically complex sentence (see notes to the transcription and translation).

§24 *Disparagement.* Although insults were a feature of academic and polemical discourse at the time, Luther is especially fond of them in his popular vernacular writing.[163] They may be expressed through word choice (e.g. 'plauderey' L9, 'geplerre' L20), but can also involve sustained invective; thus the *Sermon* ends with a colourful swipe at Luther's scholastic opponents, portraying them as sinister, ignorant, washed-out relics.

§25 *Proverbs and sayings.* Luther often lightens his writing with proverbs – or at least proverb-like statements, because it is sometimes not possible to tell whether he is reusing an existing proverb or coining one himself. Examples in the *Sermon* are: 'Es ist besser eyn gutes werck gethā / dañ vill nach gelassen', '[er] sucht yhe dein seel

[163] On the relative frequency of insults in Luther's writings and those of his contemporaries, see Franzjosef Pensel, Zur Personalabwertung, in: Gerhard Kettmann and Joachim Schildt (eds), Zur Literatursprache im Zeitalter der frühbürgerlichen Revolution. Untersuchungen zu ihrer Verwendung in der Agitationsliteratur, Berlin 1978, 219–340, especially 339.

in deynem Beutell vnd fund er pfenning darinne / das were ym lieber dañ all seelẽ (both L16).[164]

§26 *Doublets and lists.* Luther often uses two co-ordinated synonyms or near synonyms (in line with chancery practice), possibly for emphasis; examples from the *Sermon* are 'duldet vnnd zuleszet' (L14) and 'gelassen vñ erleubt' (L17).[165] On the other hand he is fond of asyndetic lists, e.g. 'die rew / die peycht / die gnugthuung' (L1); 'wachen / erbeiten / hart lager / cleider &c' (L3); and 'tzu den kirchen / altarn / schmuck / kelich' (L16). Such lists, especially those ending 'etc.' (L3, 6), add pace to the text and sound spontaneous.

§27 *Modal particles.* These are unstressed words which convey, in general terms, the speaker's attitude to what is being said. As in NHG, they were part of the language of persuasion in Luther's time and avoided in formal writing,[166] and it is a reasonable assumption that they were characteristic of the spoken language. They are not widely used in the *Sermon*, but examples with *doch* and *ja* include 'so doch' ('when in fact') (L13) and 'ya alls was … ' ('Indeed everything which … ') (L9).

We may wonder at the mix of stylistic features in the *Sermon*: homiletic in 16, with its clear instruction and imaginary question and

---

[164] See James C. Cornette, Proverbs and Proverbial Expressions in the German Works of Martin Luther, ed. by Wolfgang Mieder and Dorothee Racette, Bern 1997.

[165] See Neil R. Leroux, Luther's use of doublets in: Rhetoric Society Quarterly 30 (2000), 35–54.

[166] See Joachim Schildt, Modalwörter – Aufkommen und Verbreitung in Texten des 16. Jahrhunderts, in: Peter Wiesinger (ed.), Studien zum Frühneuhochdeutschen. Emil Skála zum 60. Geburtstag, Göppingen 1988, 247–62; and Peter von Polenz, Deutsche Sprachgeschichte vom Spätmittelalter bis zur Gegenwart. 1: Einführung – Grundbegriffe – 14. bis 16. Jahrhundert, Berlin/New York ^{2}2000, 247–48.

answer; densely reasoned in 8, in which much of Luther's argument is distilled into a few lines; disparaging in 20, with its comic portrayal of the wretches opposing him. But this was no ordinary sermon. Judging from its title it was preached at Wittenberg, but it was above all meant as an opportunity for Luther to set out his views on indulgences for a general audience (see 'Theological and Historical Background'). In its style no less than in its subject matter, the *Sermon* set a precedent, and set the tone, for a stream of works in which Luther would give the reading and listening public access to the central arguments of the Reformation.

A note on the translations in this edition

The translations of the *Sermon* and of the *95 Theses* are primarily meant as an aid to understand the original alongside. In the translation of the *Sermon* an attempt has also been made to convey in English something of Luther's style.

These translations, as well as the analysis of Luther's language and style (above), benefited enormously from perceptive comments and suggestions by Jeffrey Ashcroft, John Flood, Shami Ghosh, Lucas Jones, Martin Jones, Henrike Lähnemann, Martin Keßler, Nigel Palmer, Charles Russ, and Edmund Wareham, to all of whom I am extremely grateful.

Ill. 17: Arch. 8° G. 1518 (5)
(Basel edition)

Ill. 18: Arch. 8° G. 1518 (6)
(Leipzig edition)

Taylor Institution Library upper pastedown of the two copies of the *Sermon von Ablass und Gnade*. For an explanation of the various coats of arms and previous and current shelfmarks featured, cf. chapter 2.1. Acquisition, liii–lvi.

Martin Luther

Sermon von Ablass und Gnade

Sermon on Indulgences and Grace

The text is based on the Leipzig print, reproduced in this edition as the right-hand facsimile, Taylor Institution Library, Arch. 8° G. 1518 (6) [Leipzig: Valentin Schumann 1518]. Translation and annotation by Howard Jones.

The borders on this page are from the title-page of the edited copy.

Eyn Sermon von dem Ablaß vnnd gnade durch den wirdigeñ doctorñ Martinū Luther Augustiner zu Wittēbergk gemacht.[167]

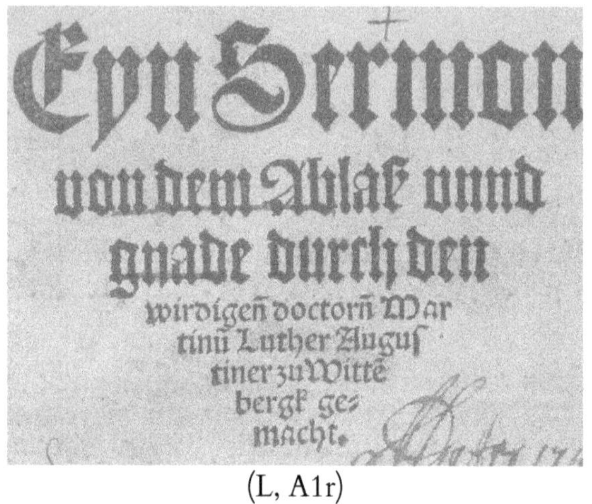
Eyn Sermon
von dem Ablaß vnnd
gnade durch den
wirdigeñ doctorñ Mar
tinū Luther Augus
tiner zu Wittē
bergk ge=
macht.

(L, A1r)

(A1v) Eyn Sermon von dem Ablaß vnnd gnade / durch deñ wirdigeñ doctorñ Martinum Luther Augustiner zu Wittenbergk geprediget.

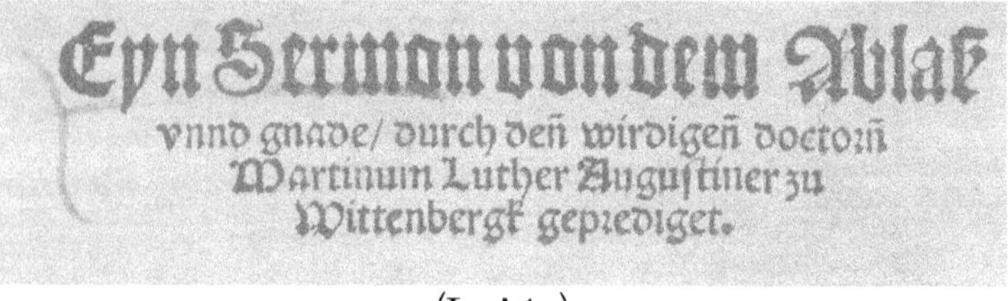
Eyn Sermon von dem Ablaß
vnnd gnade/ durch deñ wirdigeñ doctorñ
Martinum Luther Augustiner zu
Wittenbergk geprediget.

(L, A1v)

[167] The Basel print has 'gemacht vnd geprediget' both here and on the title which immediately follows. Illustrations in the transcription from the Leipzig print which is edited here are marked (L), from the Basel print (B).

A Sermon on Indulgences and Grace Composed by the Esteemed Doctor Martin Luther of the Augustinian Order, Wittenberg

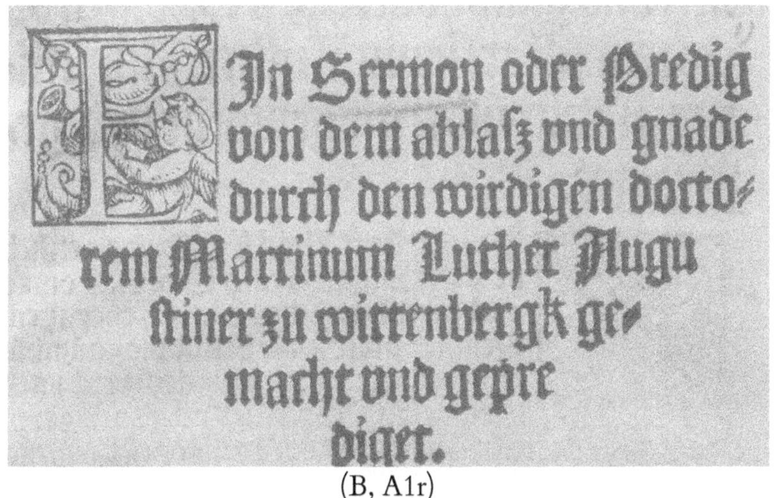

In Sermon oder Predig
von dem ablaß vnd gnade
durch den wirdigen docto-
rem Martinum Luther Augu
stiner zu wittenbergk ge-
macht vnd gepre
diget.

(B, A1r)

A Sermon on Indulgences and Grace Preached by the Esteemed Doctor Martin Luther of the Augustinian Order, Wittenberg.

Ein Sermon oder Predig võ dem ab
laß vnd gnade durch den wirdigen do
ctorem Martinum Luther Augusti-
ner zu wittenbergk gemacht vnd ge-
prediget.

(B, A1v)

¶ Czum Ersten solt yr wissen / das eczlich[168] new lerer / als[169] Magister Sentē .S. Thomas vñ yhre folger gebē d' pusz[170] drey[171] teyl / Nemlich die rew / die peycht / die gnugthuung[172] / Vñ wiewol diszer vnderscheyd[173] nach yrer meynung / schwerlich adder[174] auch gar nichts[175] / gegrundet erfunden[176] wirt in der heyligenn schrifft / noch[177] in den alten heyligen Christlichen lererñ / doch wollē wir das yctzszo[178] lassen bleyben / vnd nach yrher weysz reden.

---

[168] The spelling ‹cz› represents [ts] (see 'How to Read the *Sermon*', 5); the word is the reflex of MHG *eteslich* with syncope; the form 'etlich' (9) is the reflex (also with syncope) of the variant MHG form *etelich*. Over time, ‹cz› is replaced by ‹z› in Luther's writings.
[169] = NHG *wie*; see §19 (paragraph references are to 'Language and Style' in the Introduction).
[170] Initial ‹p› instead of ‹b› here and in 'peycht' later in the sentence reflects a pronunciation associated particularly with Bavarian, which influenced the spelling of East Central German texts at this time.
[171] The spellings ‹ey› and ‹ei› can be taken as interchangeable; over time ‹ei› comes to prevail in Luther's writings.
[172] On ‹gn›, see §1; on ‹th›, see §4.
[173] MHG had the forms *underscheit* (of which this is the reflex) and *underschiet* (of which NHG *Unterschied* is the reflex).
[174] = NHG *oder*; this word also appears with ‹o›, e.g. in 9; the spelling with ‹dd› here is consistent with a preceding vowel probably pronounced short at this time (see §§3 and 12).
[175] = NHG *nicht*; *nicht* and *nichts* were to some extent interchangeable in ENHG.
[176] = MHG *gefunden*; but see 9, where it means NHG *erfunden*.
[177] *noch* 'nor' can occur even without a preceding *weder* in ENHG.
[178] = NHG *jetzt so*; on the lack of spacing, see 'How to Read the *Sermon*, 7'; on initial ‹y›, see §14.

1. You should know that several recent teachers, such as the *Magister Sententiarum* Peter Lombard, St Thomas Aquinas, and their followers divide penance into three parts, namely contrition, confession, satisfaction.[179] And although it is scarcely, if at all, possible to find a basis for this distinction of theirs in Holy Scripture or the ancient holy Christian teachers, we shall nevertheless pass over this for now and discuss the matter in their terms.[180]

[179] Peter Lombard (1096–1160) and Thomas Aquinas (1225–74). Peter Lombard's title of *Magister Sententiarum* ('Master of Sentences') refers to his work *The Four Books of Sentences*, still a standard theology textbook in Luther's time. On the theological background to the *Sermon*, see Introduction.

[180] In the German version each point is introduced by an ordinal number written in words ('Firstly' to 'Twentiethly'). These words are sometimes integrated grammatically into the point itself by being followed immediately by a finite verb (as in 'Czum Neunden / Sag ich … ', literally: 'Ninthly say I … '). Since this type of inversion is not possible in modern English we simply number the points '1' to '20'.

¶ Czum andernñ[181] sagen[182] sie / der ablasz[183] nympt[184] nycht hynn das erst adder ander teyll / das ist / die rew adder peycht / sunderū[185] das dritt / nemlich die gnugthuung.

¶ Czum Driten. die gnugthuung wirt weyter geteylet in drey teil[186] / das ist / Beeten[187] / vastē / almuszē / also / das beetē begreyfft allerlei werck der seelē[188] eygē / als leszē / tichten[189] / horen[190] gottes wort / predigen / leeren vnd d'gleichen. Uasten begreiff allerlei werck der casteyūg seins fleyschs / als[191] wachen / erbeiten[192] / hart[193] lager[194] / cleider &c. Almuszē begreyff allerlei gute werck[195] der lyeb vñ barmherczickeyt gegen dem nehsten.[196]

---

[181] *ander* co-existed with *zweit-* in ENHG as the word for 'second'.

[182] 'sagten' in B.

[183] The clause starting 'der ablasz' is an unintroduced subordinate clause; see §20.

[184] On ‹p›, see §6.

[185] The print clearly has ‹ū›, which must be a mistake for ‹n›.

[186] On the placement of such elements outside the verbal bracket, see §22.

[187] On ‹ee›, see §2.

[188] On the weak ending, see §16.

[189] = NHG *dichten*; the spelling with ‹d› (adopted in NHG) reflects the derivation of this word from Latin *dictare*.

[190] On the non-marking of umlaut in this print, see §8.

[191] = NHG *wie*.

[192] = NHG *arbeiten*, with umlaut of [a] > [e] conditioned by the following [ei]; this is a characteristically East Central German form; cf. 'arbeiten' in B.

[193] For the lack of inflectional ending, see §16.

[194] 'ligē' 'lying' in B.

[195] For the lack of inflectional ending, see §16.

[196] Note dative after *gegen* as opposed to accusative in NHG.

2. They say that indulgences do not take away the first or second parts, that is, contrition or confession, but the third, namely satisfaction.

3. Satisfaction is further divided into three parts, which are prayer, fasting, almsgiving.[197] Thus, prayer includes all manner of works proper to the soul, such as devotional reading and writing, listening to the word of God, preaching, teaching, and the like. Fasting includes all types of work requiring mortification of one's flesh, such as vigils, toil, a hard bed and clothes, etc. Almsgiving includes all types of good work involving love and charity towards one's neighbour.

---

[197] These three parts are taken from the Sermon on the Mount (Matthew 6: 1–18).

¶ Czum Uierden[198] / Jst bey yhn allē vngeczweyfelt[199] / das der ablas hin nympt die selben werck der gnugthuūg / vor[200] die sund schuldig czuthun[201] adder auffgeseczt / dannn[202] szo[203] er die selben werck solt all hin nehmen / blieb nichts gutes mehr da / das wir thun mochtenn.[204]

(A2r) ¶ Czum Funfften. Jst bey vielē gewest[205] eyn groſſe vñ noch vnbeschloszene opiny[206] / Ab[207] der ablas auch etwas mehr hynnehme / dañ[208] solche auffgelegte gute werck / nemlich / ab er auch die peyne / die die gotlich gerechtigkeyt / vor die sunde / fordert / abnehme.

---

[198] In this ordinal number, as well as in *sibende* and others ending *-nde*, ‹d› > ‹t› between ENHG and NHG by analogy with ordinal numbers such as *erste-, dritte-, fünfte-*. The ‹d› in 'Uierden' dates back to Old High German (*fiordo*), and in those ending *-nde* to MHG.

[199] 'vngeczweyflet' in B; the ending would originally have been *-elet*, and the two prints reflect syncope of different unstressed vowels (see §1).

[200] = NHG *für*; see §19.

[201] 'schuldig czuthun' qualifies 'sund' and means 'due (to be done)'; this sense of *schuldig* is not found in NHG.

[202] On ‹nnn›, see §3.

[203] 'if'; see §19.

[204] Here = NHG *könnten.*

[205] This form of the past participle as well as *gewesen* occurred across the High German dialect areas at this time.

[206] This loan word from Latin *opinio* is rarely attested in ENHG.

[207] = *ob*; see §§12 and 19.

[208] = NHG *als*; see §19.

4. None of them doubts that indulgences take away those works of satisfaction which we are bound to do, or which are imposed on us, for sin.[209] For if indulgences were to take away these works altogether, there would be no good left that we could do.

5. Among many of them there has been a strongly held opinion – and it is still not decided – about whether indulgences take away more than those good works which are imposed, that is, whether they also take away the punishment[210] which God's righteousness demands for sin.

---

[209] Luther is referring here to temporal penalties imposed by the church either according to canon law or, if the sin was not explicitly provided for in canon law, at the discretion of the confessor.

[210] The word 'peyn(e)', which has the sense of both 'punishment' and 'suffering', has been translated as 'punishment' throughout the *Sermon*; cf. thesis 4 in the *95 Theses* and the note to it in this edition.

¶ Czum Sechsten. Lasz ich yhre opiny vnuorworffeñ auff das[211] mal / Das sag ich / das mā ausz keyner schrifft bewerenn kañ / das gottlich gerechtigkeyt etwas peyn adder gnugthuung begere adder fordere[212] / vonn dem sunder. Dañ[213] allein seyne herczliche vnd ware rew adder bekerūg myt vorsacz hynfurder[214] / das Creucz Christi[215] czu tragenn / vnnd die obgenanten werck (auch von nyemāt auffgeseczt) czu vben / Dañ szo[216] spricht er durch Ezechie. Man[217] sich der sunder bekeret / vñ thut recht / so will ich seyner sunde nicht mehr gedencken. Jtem also hatt er selbs[218] all die absoluirt.[219] Maria Magda.[220] den gichtpruchtigē.[221] Die eebrecherynne &c. Uñd mocht[222] woll[223] gerne horen wer das anders bewerē soll. Unangesehen das eczlich doctores[224] szo gedaucht[225] haben.

---

[211] 'disz' in B.

[212] On the use of the subjunctive, see §20.

[213] Here = 'except'.

[214] = NHG *fürderhin.*

[215] A Latin genitive singular ending; see §18.

[216] 'also' in B.

[217] Comparison with 'M'aria 'M'agda. later in this point shows that there is indeed an 'M' in 'Man'. The spelling may be deliberate, as *wan* (here = NHG *wenn*) is sometimes spelt *man* in ENHG; alternatively it could be a mistake, or the printer might have run out of the rare letter 'W' (the only genuine 'W' in the text occurs in 'Wittenbergk' in the title). B has 'wan'.

[218] On the absence of final ‹t›, see §5.

[219] Note that Luther uses a loan word here (from Latin *absolvēre*) for a technical theological term for which there was no native equivalent.

[220] = 'Magdalena'.

[221] = NHG *gichtbrüchig.*

[222] The personal pronoun 'ich' is omitted before 'mocht' (= NHG *ich möchte*); this sometimes occurs in ENHG when the pronoun is obvious in context.

[223] On the meaning of 'wol', see §19.

[224] A Latin nominative plural ending; see §18.

[225] On this form, see §17.

6. I will put off a rebuttal of their opinion for the time being, and I will say only this:[226] It cannot be proved from any part of Holy Scripture that divine righteousness desires or demands any punishment or satisfaction from sinners except only for their heartfelt and true contrition, or their turning away,[227] with the intention of bearing the cross of Christ[228] and performing the above-mentioned works from then on (even if not imposed by anyone). For, as He says through Ezekiel, 'If the sinner turns away and does right, I will no longer remember his sin'.[229] And likewise there are all those He absolved Himself: Mary Magdalene, the man sick with palsy, the woman taken in adultery, etc.[230] And I would very much like to hear anyone prove otherwise – regardless of the fact that quite a few doctors of theology have supposed this.

---

226 Luther offers more arguments against this claim in the *95 Theses*; see, for example, theses 20, 26, and 28.

227 i.e. from sin.

228 See Matthew 16: 24.

229 This is a paraphrase of Ezekiel 18: 21–22.

230 The three episodes referred to can be found in Luke 7: 36–50, Mark 2: 1–12, and John 8: 1–11, respectively. The first episode tells of the anointing of Jesus by a woman who is not named but was traditionally taken to be Mary Magdalene.

¶ Czum Sibenden. Das findet man woll / das gott eczlich nach seyner gerechtigkeyt straffet / Ader durch peyne dringt czu der rew / wie ym .88. p̄s.[231] Szo seyn kinder werden sundigen[232] / will ich myt der ruthen[233] / yhre sunde heym suchen / Aber doch meyn barmherczickeyt nit[234] vonn yhnn[235] wendē. Aber disze peyne / stehet in nyemandes gewalt nachczulassen / dann̄ alleyne gottis.[236] Ja er will sie nit lassen / sūder vorspricht[237] / er woll sie aufflegē.[238]

¶ Czum Achten. Der halbē[239] szo kann man der selbē gedunckten peyn / keynen namen geben / weysz[240] auch nyemant / was sye ist / szo[241] sie disze straff nyt ist. auch dye guten / obgenanten werck nit ist.

Aij

[231] Abbreviation for 'Psalm' (abbreviated to 'Psal.' in B).
[232] 'sünden' in B.
[233] For this weak ending, see §16.
[234] This form represents *nicht* with weak speech stress; both forms are found in this text; in Luther's later writings *nicht* predominates.
[235] = NHG *ihnen*.
[236] The spelling ‹i› for the unstressed vowel [ə] is associated particularly with the Central German dialect area in ENHG.
[237] On *vor*- rather than *ver*-, see §13.
[238] 'er woll sie aufflegē' is an unintroduced subordinate clause; see §20.
[239] = NHG *deshalb*; this and the following 'szo' are both adverbs meaning 'for this reason'.
[240] According to NHG grammar we should expect an expletive 'es' before 'weysz' to ensure that the finite verb is the second constituent in the clause.
[241] The word order which follows, with the finite verb in final position, tells us that this is a subordinate clause (with 'szo' meaning 'if' here).

7. It is true that God does punish several people according to His righteousness, or through punishment forces them to contrition, as in Psalm 88: 'If his children sin, I will punish their sins with the rod, yet I will still not turn my mercy away from them'.[242] But the power to set aside this punishment belongs to no-one but God alone. In fact He does not wish to set it aside but affirms that He wishes to impose it.[243]

8. So therefore it is impossible to give a name to that supposed punishment, and no-one knows what it is, if it is not the punishment just mentioned nor the good works referred to above.[244]

---

[242] Psalm 88: 31–34 (Vulgate); Psalm 89: 30–33 (King James Version). Luther appears to misquote the Psalm, which has 'him' rather than 'them' (including in Luther's own Bible translations).

[243] Luther is using Psalm 88 as an example in which God *does* choose to punish sin according to His righteousness.

[244] Luther's point here is that, since the divinely imposed punishment mentioned in 5, which is supposed to be cancelled by indulgences, is neither the punishment in 7 nor the good works in 3, it cannot be identified.

(A2v) ¶ Czum Neunden. Sag ich / ob[245] die Christenliche kirch noch heut beschlusz / vnd ausz ercleret / das[246] der ablas mehr dañ die werck der gnugthuūg hyn neme[247] / szo were es den nocht[248] tausentmal besser / das keyn Christen mensch den ablas loszet oder begeret / sunderñ das sye lieber die werck thetten vnnd die peyn litten / dañ der ablas / nit anderst ist nach[249] mag werden / dañ nachlassung gutter werck / vnnd heylsamer peyn / die man billich solt erwellē dañn vorlassen / wiewol etlich d′ newen prediger zweyerley peyne erfunden[250] / Medicatiuas Satisfactorias[251] / das ist etzlich peyn czur der gnugthuūg / eczlich czur der[252] besserung / Aber wir haben mehr freyheyt czuuorachten[253] (got lob)[254] sulchs[255] vnnd des gleychen plauderey / dañ sie haben czu ertichten / dañn alle peyn / ya[256] alls was got auff legt / ist besserlich vnd tzu treglich[257] den Christen.

---

[245] = NHG *auch wenn* 'even if'; see §19.

[246] In NHG syntax, 'das' (= *dass*) would immediately follow 'Sag ich' at the beginning of the sentence; in ENHG the delayed position, which avoids the nesting of one subordinate clause in another, is not uncommon.

[247] 'beschlusz', 'ausz ercleret', and 'hyn neme' are preterite subjunctives (their NHG equivalents are *beschlösse, auserklärte,* and *hinnähme*), as are 'loszet', 'begeret', 'thetten', and 'litten' later in the sentence.

[248] On final ‹t›, see §5.

[249] = *noch*; see §12.

[250] Preterite plural of *erfinden* (NHG *erfanden*).

[251] Latin accusative feminine plural endings; see §18.

[252] Note the pleonastic 'czur' (= *zu der*) + 'der'.

[253] Note that 'czuuorachten' (NHG *zu verachten*) would occur after the object 'plauderey' in NHG.

[254] 'got zů lob' in B.

[255] The spelling with ‹u› is characteristic of East Central German (cf. 'solichs' in B); 'sulchs' and 'des' are genitive singulars with the substantival adjective 'gleychen'; cf. English *suchlike*.

[256] A modal particle; see §27.

[257] 'zůtrå̈glicher' in B.

9. I will say this, that even if the Christian church decided and proclaimed today that indulgences took away more than the works of satisfaction, it would still be a thousand times better if not one Christian bought an indulgence or wanted one, and that they preferred to perform works and suffer punishment instead. For indulgences are nothing, and can become nothing, other than a setting aside of the good works and salutary punishment which one would do better to embrace than avoid – even though some of the recent preachers have invented two kinds of punishments, 'medicativae' and 'satisfactoriae', that is, some for satisfaction and some for improvement.[258] But we are, praise God, more at liberty to ignore this sort of prattle than they are to make it up: all punishment, indeed everything that God burdens us with, is for the improvement and benefit of Christians.

---

[258] Luther is referring to Johann Tetzel and Konrad Wimpina whose 106 theses, which were a response to Luther's *95 Theses*, were publicly defended at the University of Frankfurt an der Oder on 15 January 1518. In those theses, Tetzel and Wimpina argue for the distinction between rehabilitation ('medicativae') and retribution ('satisfactoriae') which Luther attacks here. See Introduction, p. xxxiv.

¶ Czū czehenden / Das ist nichts[259] geredt / das der peyn vnnd werck czu vill[260] seynn[261] / das der mensch sye nit mag vol brengen[262] / der kurcz halben[263] seyns lebens / Darumb[264] yhm nott sey der Ablas. Antwort ich das / das kein grundt[265] hab / vñ eyn lauter geticht[266] ist / Dañ gott vnnd die heylige kirche / legen nyemand mehr auff / dañ yhm[267] czu tragē muglich[268] ist / als auch. S. Paul sagt / das got nit leszt vorsucht werden yemand / mehr dañ er mag tragen / vnd es langet[269] nit wenig czu der Christenheyt schmach[270] / Das mā yhr schuld gibt / sye lege auff mehr / dañ wir tragen kunen.[271]

---

259 Here = NHG *nicht*.

260 'der peyn vnnd werck' are partitive genitives dependent on 'czu vill'; see §21.

261 This could represent NHG *sind* (indicative) or NHG *seien* (subjunctive); see §§17 and 20.

262 Vowel lowering (here of [i] to [ɛ]) is characteristic of Central German; cf. 'volbringen' in B. This and the lowering of [u] > [o] and of [ü] > [ö] were conditioned particularly by a following nasal or *l*/*r* + consonant; see notes to 'sunst' in 13 and 'furdert' in 14.

263 = NHG *halber*.

264 Given the delayed position of the verb in this clause, we can take 'Darumb' as an adverbial relative ('for which reason'; = NHG *worum*) rather than as a demonstrative ('for that reason').

265 On ‹dt›, see §4.

266 In ENHG this could refer generally to something made up, not just a poem as in NHG *Gedicht*.

267 B has the plural 'yn' here rather than the singular.

268 Forms of this word with ‹u› or, reflecting lowering before a nasal, with ‹o› co-existed in a number of dialect areas; similarly 'kunen' a few lines below.

269 NHG *langen* no longer has this sense; a semantic equivalent is *gereichen*.

270 On the order of noun and dependent genitive, see §21.

271 'sye ... kunen' is an unintroduced subordinate clause; see §20. B has 'moͤgen' rather than 'kunen'.

10. This is not to say that punishments and works are excessive, that nobody can complete them because of the shortness of life, and so they need indulgences.[272] My response is that this is unfounded and a pure fabrication. For God and the holy Church do not burden anyone with more than is bearable for them. As St Paul also says, God does not allow anyone to be tested beyond what they can endure,[273] and it is no small disgrace to Christianity that it is accused of burdening us with more than we can bear.

---

[272] Here Luther is attacking another claim made in Tetzel's and Wimpina's 106 theses.

[273] 1 Corinthians 10: 13.

¶ Czum eylfften.[274] Wann gleych[275] die pusz ym geystlichē recht geseczt / iczt[276] noch ginge[277] / Das vor ein yglich todtsund / syeben iar pusz auffgelegt were / Szo must doch die Christenheyt / dye selbē gesecz lassen / vñ nit weyter aufflegen / dañ sye eynem yglichen[278] czu tragē warē.[279] Uil weniger / nu[280] sye iczt nicht seyn / sall[281] mā achtē[282] / das nicht mehr auffgelegt werde[283] dañ yederman wol tragē kan.

---

[274] = NHG *elften*; cf. MHG *einlif* 'eleven'.

[275] = NHG *wenngleich*.

[276] = NHG *jetzt*; see §14.

[277] On the use of the subjunctive; see §20. B has the plural 'gingen' here; 'die pusz' could be singular or plural (see §16).

[278] 'jetlichen' in B.

[279] = NHG *wären*.

[280] = 'now that'; B has 'so ... nun'.

[281] On the spelling with ‹a›, see §12.

[282] B has 'so soll man achtē / das meer' instead of 'sall mā achtē / das nicht mehr'.

[283] On the use of the subjunctive, see §20.

11. Even if the penitential rules laid down in canon law were still in force today, which imposed seven years' penance for each mortal sin, Christianity would still have to waive these laws and not enforce them beyond what is bearable for each person. Far less, now that these rules are no longer in force, should one think of burdening anyone with more than they can readily bear.[284]

[284] The Leipzig print has 'nicht' ('not') here, which would give the sense, 'Far less, … , should one think of not imposing … '. This has been omitted in translation.

(A3r) ¶ Czum czwelfftē.[285] Man sagt wol / das der sunder mit der vberingen[286] peyn inszfegfewr[287] oder czum ablas geweyset sall werdenn / aber es wirt wol mehr dings[288] / an[289] grundt vnd bewerung gesagt.

¶ Czum Dreyczehendē. Es ist eyn groszer yrthū das yemādt meyne / er wolle gnugthun vor seyne sundt / so doch got die selbē alczeyt vmb sunst[290] / ausz vnscheczlicher gnad vorczeyhet / nichts darfur begerend / dā hynfurder woll leben.[291] Die Christenheyt fordert wol etwas / also mag sie vnd sall auch das selb nachlassen / vnnd nichts schweres adder vntreglichs auflegen.

---

[285] On the spelling with ‹e›, see §11.

[286] = NHG *übrigen*; the insertion of ‹n› may reflect colloquial pronunciation.

[287] = 'insz fegfewr'; on the lack of spacing, see 'How to Read the *Sermon*, 7'.

[288] A partitive genitive (see §21); lit. 'more of thing'.

[289] In ENHG *an*(*e*), ‹a› = [a:]; this was later raised and rounded to [o:] in NHG *ohne*.

[290] = NHG *umsonst*; on ‹b›, see §6; for the later lowering of [u] to [o], see note to *brengen* in 10 above.

[291] NHG would have *zu leben*.

12. People certainly claim that sinners with punishment still outstanding should be shown the way towards purgatory or towards indulgences, but a great deal more is also claimed which is without foundation and proof.

13. It is a grave error for anyone to think that they should aim to make satisfaction for their sins, when in fact God in His unfathomable grace always forgives those sins for free, desiring nothing in return except to live a good life from then on. Christianity does make demands of its own, so it can and should set these aside as well, rather than burdening people with anything harsh or unbearable.

¶ Czum Uierczehendē. Ablasz wirt czu gelassen vmb der vnuolkōmen vnd faulen Christeu[292] willen / die sich nit wollen kecklich[293] vben in guten wercken / oder vnleydlich seyn / dañ ablas furdert[294] nyeman czum bessern / sundern duldet vnnd zuleszet yr vnuolkōmen[295] / darumb soll man nit wider das[296] ablas redenn / man sall aber auch nyemand darczu[297] reden.

¶ Czum Funffczehenden. Uill sicherer / vnnd besserer[298] thet der / der lauter vmb gottes willen / gebe czu dē gebewde .S. Petri[299] / ader was sunst genāt wirt / Dan das er ablasz darfur nehme[300] / dañ[301] es ferlich[302] ist / das er sulch gabe vmb desz ablas[303] willē vñ nit vmb gotts willē gibt

[292] 'Christeu' seems to be a clear error for 'Christen'.

[293] 'lively'; etymologically related to Engl *quick*.

[294] = *fürdert*; for the later lowering of [ü] to [ö] as in NHG *fördert*, see note to *brengen* in 10 above.

[295] = NHG *Unvollkommenheit* (as it appears in B).

[296] The noun was masculine or rarely, as here, neuter, in ENHG.

[297] = NHG *dazu*; the construction is not found in NHG and is equivalent to *niemandem dazu raten* or *niemandem in dieser Sache zureden*.

[298] Note the redundant *-er*.

[299] Abbreviation for 'Sancti Petri', a Latin genitive singular; see §18; cf. 'sanct Peters' with a German genitive ending in 16.

[300] 'thet … gebe … nehme' are preterite subjunctives (= NHG *täte … gäbe … nähme*).

[301] Note that the causal conjunction 'dañ' is followed by subordinate-clause word order here.

[302] ≈ NHG *gefährlich*.

[303] For lack of genitive singular ending, see §1.

14. Indulgences are permitted for the sake of those imperfect and idle Christians who are none too keen to do good works or cannot bear suffering, for indulgences do not help people to improve, but tolerate and condone imperfection in them, so while one should not speak against indulgences, one should not recommend them to anyone either.

15. If one were to make a donation for the building of St Peter's or for whatever other cause is proposed, it would be far safer and better to do so purely for God's sake than to take an indulgence for it, for it is unsafe to make a gift like that for the sake of an indulgence and not for God.

¶ Czum Secheczehendē.[304] Uill besser ist das werck eynen[305] durfftigen erczeygt / dan das czum gebewde geben[306] wirt auch vill besser / dan der ablas dafur gegebē / dan wie gesagt. Es ist besser eyn gutes werck gethā / dañ vill nach gelassen. Ablas aber / ist nachlassung villgutter werck / ader ist nichts nach gelassen.
(A3v) Ja[307] das ich euch recht vnderweise. szo merckt auff / du salt[308] vor allenn dingen (widder[309] sanct Peters gebewde noch ablas angesehen) deynē nehsten armē geben / wiltu[310] etwas geben. Wañ esz aber dahyn kumpt[311] / das nyemandt yn deyner stat mehr ist der hulff[312] bedarff (das ob gotwill nymer gescheen[313] sall) dañ saltu geben szo du wilt tzu den kirchen / altarn / schmuck / kelich[314] / die in deyner stat seyn. Und wen das auch nu nit mehr not ist / Dañ aller erst / szo du wilt / magstu geben zu dē gebewde. S. Peters adder anderwo.

Aiij

304 The ‹e› in the middle of 'Sech<u>e</u>czehendē' is unhistoric and does not appear in B or in the Wittenberg prints.
305 We should expect the dative 'einem' here; the nasal bar in B ('einē') could stand for ‹n› or ‹m›, and ‹n› here may be an error.
306 = 'gegeben'.
307 B has 'Aber' here.
308 = NHG *sollst* and later 'wilt' = NHG *willst*; [s] was added by analogy with verbs whose second person singular ended -*st* (already in 'magstu' below). Note the switch from second-person plural to second-person singular between 'merckt' and 'salt'.
309 = NHG *weder*, often spelt with an ‹i› in Luther's early writings; the spelling with ‹dd› here is consistent with a preceding vowel probably pronounced short in both *weder* and *wider* at this time (see §3).
310 On contracted forms, see §7.
311 On ‹p›, see §6.
312 ENHG texts show widespread variation: *helfe, hilfe, hülfe* (B: 'hilff').
313 The omission of ‹h› here suggests that it was no longer pronounced in medial position, which is consistent with its use as a length marker; see §2.
314 = NHG *Kelch*; an early loan word from Latin *calix* with umlaut of [a] > [e].

16. Far better is the work done for someone in need than as a donation for a building, and far better than the indulgence given for it since, as stated before, one good work done is better than many avoided. Yet indulgences *are* the avoidance of many good works if they are the avoidance of anything. Now pay attention so that I can give you clear instructions: If you want to make a gift, you should do so first and foremost (leaving aside the building of St Peter's and indulgences) to a neighbour in need. But if it comes to the point that there is no-one left in your town who needs help – which, God willing, is never going to happen – then, if you wish to make a donation, you must make one for the churches, altars, ornaments, chalices in your town. And if there is no longer a need for that either, then, and only then, if you wish, may you give something for the building of St Peter's or elsewhere.

Auch soltu dannochnit das vmb ablas willen thun. dann̄[315] sant Paul spricht Wer seynē hausz genoszē nit wol thut / ist keyn Christē vnd erger dañ ein heyde / vñ halts[316] dafur frey / wer dir ādere sagt / der vorfurt dich / adder sucht yhe[317] dein seel in deynem Beutell vnd fund[318] er pfenning darinne / das were[319] ym lieber dañ all seelē. Szo sprichttu.[320] Szo werd ich nymer mehr ablas loszen. Antwort ich / das hab ich schon obē gesagt / Das meyn will / begirde / bitt vñ ratt ist / das nyemandt ablas losze / lasz die faulen vnd schlefferigen Christen / ablas loszen / gang[321] du fur dich.

¶ Czum Sibenczehenden. Der ablas ist nich[322] geboten auch nicht geratē / sunderñ von der dinger czall[323] / die czu gelassen vñ erleubt[324] werdē. darumb ist es nit eyn werck des gehorsams / auch nit vordinstlich[325] / sunderñ eyn ausz czug des gehorsams. Darumb wiewol man / nyemant weren[326] soll / den czu loszen / szo solt mā doch alle Christē daruon cziehen / and zu den wercken vñ peynen / die do nachgelassen[327] reyczen vnd sterckenñ.

---

315 Note the redundant abbreviation; see 'How to Read the *Sermon*, 2'.

316 = 'halt es'.

317 The function of ‹h› here may be to indicate that the following, rather than the preceding, vowel is long (cf. §2).

318 For this form, see §17.

319 According to NHG word order, 'were' (= NHG *wäre*) would occur first in this clause; in ENHG it was usual not to invert subject and verb when a main clause followed a subordinate clause.

320 Note that ‹s› is missing here; cf. 'sprichst du' in B.

321 A widespread form of the imperative singular of *gehen* in ENHG.

322 On lack of final ‹t›, see §5.

323 On the order of noun and dependent genitive, see §21.

324 The umlauted form of this verb is associated particularly with East Central German (cf. 'erloubt' in B, and see 'geleub' for NHG *glaube* in 18).

325 = NHG *verdienstvoll*.

326 = NHG *verwehren*.

327 'seyn/sind' must be understood after 'nachgelassen'; auxiliary verbs were sometimes omitted in ENHG subordinate clauses.

But even this you should not do for the sake of an indulgence. As St Paul says, 'He who does not provide for those in his own household is no Christian and is worse than an infidel'.[328] Feel free to assume that anyone who tells you otherwise deceives you or is looking for your soul in your purse, and would be happier to find a penny there than any number of souls. You will say, 'In that case I shall never buy an indulgence again'. My response: 'As I have already said above, it is my wish, desire, plea, and advice that no-one buy an indulgence. Let lazy and lie-abed Christians buy indulgences: you follow your own path.'

17. Indulgences are neither required nor recommended, but are among those things which are admissible and allowed, so an indulgence is neither an act of obedience nor meritorious, but an exemption from obedience. Therefore, even though one should not stop anyone from buying indulgences,[329] one should still pull all Christians away from them, and spur them on and strengthen them for the works and punishments which are reduced thereby.

---

[328] A slightly abbreviated quotation from 1 Timothy 5: 8.

[329] By making this claim Luther may have been trying to keep within the rules of the *Instructio summaria* against impeding the sale of indulgences; see Introduction, p. xxxvi and see thesis 73 and note.

¶ Czum Achtczehendē. Ab die seelen ausz dē fegfewr geczogen werden durch den ablas / weysz ich nit / vn̄geleub das auch noch nich / wiewol das eczlich new doctores sagen / aber ist yhn vnmuglich czubeweren / auch hat es die kirch noch nit beschlossen / darumb czu meh(A4r)rer[330] sicherheyt / vil besser ist es[331] / das du vor sie selbst bittest vn̄ wirckest / dann disz ist bewerter vn̄ ist gewisz

¶ Czum Neunczehendē. Jn dissen puncten hab ich nit czweyffel / vnnd sind[332] gnugsam inder schrifft gegrund.[333] Darumb solt ir auch keyn czweyffel haben / vn̄ last doctores Scholasticos / scholasticos[334] sein / sie sein alsampt[335] nit gnug / mit yhren opinien / das sie eyne prediget befestigenn soltenn.

---

[330] Note that *mehr* could serve as an adjective in ENHG.

[331] The clause 'darumb … es' is either a main clause in which the finite verb 'ist' is delayed or a subordinate clause in which the finite verb and pronominal subject are (unusually) inverted at the end.

[332] Note that the subject *sie* would have to be specified before 'sind' in NHG.

[333] On the omission of the ending *-et*, see §1.

[334] Latin accusative plural endings; see §18.

[335] On ‹p›, see §6.

18. Whether souls are rescued from purgatory by indulgences, I do not know, nor do I even believe it, although this is what several contemporary theologians say.[336] Yet it is impossible for them to prove this, and the church has still not decided the matter, so to be on the safe side it is better for you to pray and do works for them[337] yourself – this is, after all, more reliable and *is* certain.

19. I have no doubt about these points, which have ample foundation in Scripture. So you should have no doubt either, and you should leave scholastic theologians to be scholastic. The whole lot of them together, with their opinions, could not add anything constructive to a single sermon.

---

[336] On the doctrine which allowed indulgences to apply to souls in purgatory, see Introduction, pp. xviii–xix.
[337] i.e. souls in purgatory.

¶ Czum czwenczigsten.[338] Ab etzlich mich nu wol[339] eynen keczer[340] schelten / den[341] solch warheyt seer schedlich ist im kasten. Szo acht ich doch solch geplerre nit grosz / sintemal[342] das nit thun / dañ eczlich finster gehyrne / die die Biblien[343] nie gerochē / die Christenlichē lerer nie geleszē[344] yhr eigen lerer[345] nie vorstanden[346] / sundern in yhren lochereten[347] vnd czurissen[348] opinien vill nah vorwesen / dā hetthen sie die vorstanden szo wisten[349] sie / das sie nyemādt solten lestern / vnuorhort vñ vnuberwundē / doch got geb yhn / vnd vns rechten sinn. Amen.

¶ Getruckt[350] Nach Christ geburt
Tausent funff hundert vñ ym[351] achczehenden Jar.

---

338 Forms of this word with ‹e› and ‹a› alternate in ENHG.

339 Morphologically, 'Ab' and 'wol' should be taken together as a single conjunction like NHG *obwohl*; however, the conjunction means 'even if' rather than 'although' here.

340 'eynen keczer' is in apposition to 'mich': 'as a heretic.'

341 = NHG *denen.*

342 'since'; < MHG *sint dem mâle* 'since that time'.

343 On the weak ending, see §16.

344 The lack of punctuation is explained by the fact that 'geleszē' is followed by a line break in the print; see 'How to Read the *Sermon*, 1'.

345 B has 'lere ... leren' (NHG *Lehre(n)*) as opposed to 'lerer ... lerer' (NHG *Lehrer*) here.

346 The auxiliary verb 'haben' must be understood here.

347 = NHG *löcherig*; *löcheret* derives from MHG *löchericht* with weakening of *-icht* to *-et.*

348 = NHG *zerrissenen*; the NHG prefix *zer-* appears as *czu/zu-* or *czur/zur-* throughtout Luther's writings; on the loss of *-en*, see §1.

349 On this form, see §11.

350 Forms of this word are commonly found with initial ‹t› and ‹d› in ENHG.

351 Note that 'ym' occurs immediately before the inflected form, thus breaking up the numeral.

20. Even though I may well be branded a heretic by a number of people[352] whose coffers are seriously damaged by these truths, I don't pay much attention to such blather, especially since the only ones doing this are certain dark minds who have never been within smelling distance of the Bible, never read the Christian teachers, never understood their own teachers, but, under their tattered, threadbare opinions, are all but wasting away. For if they had understood them, they would know not to defame anyone without hearing them out or countering them. Even so, may God give them and us a right understanding! Amen.

Printed in the one thousand five hundred and eighteenth year after the birth of Christ

---

[352] See Introduction, p. xxxiv, for who these people might be.

DISPVTATIO D. MARTINI LVTHERI THEOLOGI
PRO DECLARATIONE VIRTVTIS INDVLGENTIARVM

AMORE ET STVDIO ELVCIdandæ ueritatis hæc ſubſcripta diſputabuntur Vuittenbergæ, Præſidente R.P. Martino Luther, Artium & S. Theologiæ Magiſtro, eiuſdemque ibidem lectore Ordinatio. Quare petit ut qui non poſſunt uerbis præſentes nobiſcum diſceptare, agant id literis abſentes. In nomine domini noſtri Ieſu Chriſti. Amen.

j Ominus & Magiſter noſter Ieſus Chriſtus, dicendo pœnitentiam agite &c. omnem uitam fidelium, pœnitentiam eſſe uoluit.

xxij Quin nullam remittit animabus in purgatorio, quam in hac uita debuiſſent ſecundum Canones ſoluere.

xxiij Si remiſſio ulla omnium omnino pœnarum poteſt alicui dari: certum eſt eam non niſi perfectiſſimis, .i. pauciſſimis dari.

xxiv Falli ob id neceſſe eſt, maiorem partem populi: per indifferentem illam & magnificam pœnæ ſolutæ promiſſionem.

xxv Qualem poteſtatem habet Papa in purgatorium generaliter talem habet quilibet Epiſcopus & curatus in ſua dioceſi, & parochia ſpecialiter.

xxvj Optime facit Papa, quod non poteſtate clauis (quam nullam habet) ſed per modum ſuffragii, dat animabus remiſſionem

Martin Luther

95 Theses

The text is based on the Weimar Edition (WA), vol. 1, pp. 232–38. Translation and annotation by Howard Jones.

The header art on this page is taken from the facsimile typeset by Charlotte Hartmann and students of the Faculty of Medieval and Modern Languages for the Reformation quincentenary. https://lutherinoxford.wordpress.com/2016/05/12/how-to-print-your-own-95-luther-theses/
The header of the text shown above (*Disputatio* etc.) first appears on the separate title page of the Basel edition mentioned on p. xxviii. It is not part of the broadsides the WA edition is based on and hence not included in the Latin text shown.

	Latin	Translation
	Amore et studio elucidande[353] veritatis hec subscripta disputabuntur Wittenberge, Presidente R. P. Martino Lutther, Artium et S. Theologie Magistro eiusdemque ibidem lectore Ordinario. Quare petit, ut qui non possunt verbis presentes nobiscum disceptare agant id literis absentes. In nomine domini nostri Hiesu Christi. Amen.	Out of love for the truth and a desire to bring it to light, the following will be debated at Wittenberg under the Reverend Father Martin Luther, Master of Arts and Theology, and Official Lecturer in Theology there. He therefore requests that those unable to debate with us in person should, in their absence, do so in writing. In the name of our Lord Jesus Christ. Amen.
1	Dominus et magister noster Iesus Christus dicendo 'Penitentiam agite &c.' omnem vitam fidelium penitentiam esse voluit.	When our Lord and master Jesus Christ said, 'Do penance, etc.', he meant the whole life of the faithful to be penance.[354]
2	Quod verbum de penitentia sacramentali (id est confessionis et satisfactionis, que sacerdotum ministerio celebratur) non potest intelligi.	This word cannot be understood to refer to sacramental penance (that is, confession and satisfaction as administered by the clergy).[355]
3	Non tamen solam intendit interiorem, immo interior	Nor, however, does it mean only inner penance: on the contrary, inner penance is worthless unless

[353] Final -*e* stands for -*ae*, as often in this text.

[354] 'Penitentiam agite' ('Do penance') is a quotation from Matthew 4: 17 in the Vulgate. As Luther makes clear in the *Resolutiones disputationum de indulgentiarum virtute* (see Introduction, p. xi), the Latin is a translation of the Greek μετανοεῖτε, which comes from a verb meaning 'to change one's state of mind' (it is likely that Luther found this in Erasmus's 1516 edition of the Greek New Testament). Luther's point in theses 1 and 2 is that penance should be viewed as a change in one's way of life rather than as the performance of works (see Introduction, p. xv). The Latin word *poenitentia* (spelt here 'penitentia') can be translated in English by 'penance', 'penitence', or 'repentance'; for consistency it has been translated as 'penance' here.

[355] See Introduction, p. xxvii, and *Sermon* 1.

	nulla est, nisi foris operetur varias carnis mortificationes.	it manifests itself in various mortifications of the flesh.[356]
4	Manet itaque pena, donec manet odium sui (id est penitentia vera intus), scilicet usque ad introitum regni celorum.	Punishment[357] therefore lasts for as long as hatred of the self (that is true inner penance), in other words, until entry into the kingdom of heaven.[358]
5	Papa non vult nec potest ullas penas remittere preter eas, quas arbitrio vel suo vel canonum imposuit.	The pope neither desires nor is able to remit any punishments except those which he has imposed by his own authority or that of the canons.[359]
6	Papa non potest remittere ullam culpam nisi declarando et approbando remissam a deo Aut certe remittendo casus reservatos sibi, quibus contemptis culpa prorsus remaneret.	The pope cannot remit any guilt except by declaring and affirming that it has been remitted by God or, of course, by remitting cases reserved to himself – and if such cases were disregarded, the guilt would certainly remain.[360]

[356] The idea that penance has both an inward and an outward manifestation was not new in Luther's time: it occurs in the writings of Peter Lombard (see *Sermon* 1).

[357] The Latin word *pena* (= *poena*), which has the sense of both 'punishment' and 'suffering', has been translated as 'punishment' throughout the *95 Theses*; cf. *Sermon* 5 and note.

[358] For self-hatred, see John 12: 25; for entry into the kingdom of heaven, see Matthew 7: 21–23.

[359] 'Remit' and 'remission' are technical terms for 'forgive' and 'forgiveness'. If the punishments to be imposed were not specified in the penitential canons (see thesis 8), the priest could exercise his discretion.

[360] In theses 6 and 7 Luther explains the roles of God and the pope in the remission of guilt (as opposed to punishment). In cases where God's grace is required for the remission of guilt, sinners must submit to the pope, but the pope only has the authority to confirm that God has remitted their guilt, not to remit it himself. In cases reserved to himself, the pope does have the power to remit guilt, which must be respected.

7	Nulli prorsus remittit deus culpam, quin simul eum subiiciat humiliatum in omnibus sacerdoti suo vicario.	God does not remit the guilt of anyone at all without at the same time completely humbling them and subjecting them to a priest as his representative.
8	Canones penitentiales solum viventibus sunt impositi nihilque morituris secundum eosdem debet imponi.	The penitential canons are imposed only on the living, and according to the canons nothing must be imposed on the dying.[361]
9	Inde bene nobis facit spiritus sanctus in papa excipiendo in suis decretis semper articulum mortis et necessitatis.	That is why the Holy Spirit is kind to us through the pope by always making exceptions in his decrees for the moment of death and distress.
10	Indocte et male faciunt sacerdotes ii, qui morituris penitentias canonicas in purgatorium reservant.	Priests who carry over the canonical penalties of the dying into purgatory are acting ignorantly and wickedly.
11	Zizania illa de mutanda pena Canonica in penam purgatorii videntur certe dormientibus episcopis seminata.	Those tares – the changing of canonical punishment into purgatorial punishment – were evidently sown while the bishops were asleep.[362]
12	Olim pene canonice non post, sed ante absolutionem imponebantur tanquam tentamenta vere contritionis.	Once, canonical punishments were imposed not after, but before, absolution, as tests of true contrition.[363]

[361] The penitential canons, drawn up in the Middle Ages as a guide for confessors, specified a penance for particular sins.

[362] The image is taken from the Parable of the Tares told in Matthew 13: 24–30 (a tare is a type of weed).

[363] According to church doctrine at the time, after the first two parts of penance (contrition and confession), the priest absolved the penitent, declaring that the guilt of sin was removed and that what had been an eternal penalty was made into a temporal (or 'canonical') one; it was only after this that the absolved sinner had to pay the penalty. This was the third part of penance, called satisfaction (see *Sermon* 1–3). In this thesis Luther refers to an earlier practice by which temporal penalties had to be paid before absolution.

13	Morituri per mortem omnia solvunt et legibus canonum mortui iam sunt, habentes iure earum relaxationem.	The dying pay off everything through death, and they are already dead as far as canon laws are concerned, being released from those laws by right.
14	Imperfecta sanitas seu charitas morituri necessario secum fert magnum timorem, tantoque maiorem, quanto minor fuerit ipsa.	Imperfect purity or love in a dying person necessarily brings with it great fear, and this fear is all the greater, the less their love has been.
15	Hic timor et horror satis est se solo (ut alia taceam) facere penam purgatorii, cum sit proximus desperationis horrori.	This fear, this horror is enough by itself (not to mention other things) to constitute the punishment of purgatory, since it is closest to the horror of despair.[364]
16	Videntur infernus, purgatorium, celum differre, sicut desperatio, prope desperatio, securitas differunt.	The difference between hell, purgatory, and heaven seems to be like that between despair, near-despair, and the certainty of salvation.[365]
17	Necessarium videtur animabus in purgatorio sicut minui horrorem ita augeri charitatem.	For souls in purgatory, it appears necessary that, just as their fear is reduced, so their love is increased.
18	Nec probatum videtur ullis aut rationibus aut scripturis, quod sint extra statum meriti seu augende charitatis.	And it does not seem to have been proved, either by reason or from scripture, that they are outside the

[364] According to church doctrine at the time, in purgatory the dead paid the penalties for sin which they had not paid in life, before entering heaven (see Introduction, pp. xviii–xix). In this thesis Luther argues that the real punishment of purgatory does not arise from penalties for particular sins, but from fear.

[365] The word *securitas* can have a positive or negative sense in the *95 Theses*. Here the sense is one of positive certainty, while in thesis 95 the word means a false sense of security or complacency.

		state of merit, that is, of increasing love.[366]
19	Nec hoc probatum esse videtur, quod sint de sua beatitudine certe et secure, saltem omnes, licet nos certissimi simus.	Nor does this seem to have been proved, that they are certain or confident of their own salvation, or at least not all of them, even if we ourselves are entirely certain.[367]
20	Igitur papa per remissionem plenariam omnium penarum non simpliciter omnium intelligit, sed a seipso tantummodo impositarum.	Therefore, by 'plenary remission of all punishments', the pope does not strictly mean all, but only those imposed by himself.[368]
21	Errant itaque indulgentiarum predicatores ii, qui dicunt per pape indulgentias hominem ab omni pena solvi et salvari.	So indulgence preachers who say that man is discharged by papal indulgences from all punishment and saved are wrong.
22	Quin nullam remittit animabus in purgatorio, quam in hac vita debuissent secundum Canones solvere.	Indeed, the pope does not remit to souls in purgatory any punishment which, according to the canons, they ought to have discharged in this life.
23	Si remissio ulla omnium omnino penarum potest alicui dari, certum est eam non nisi perfectissimis, i.e. paucissimis, dari.	If anyone can be granted a remission of absolutely all punishments, it can only be the most perfect, i.e. very few.

[366] The state of merit here means the state of grace in which, according to Luther, souls are gradually prepared for entry into heaven.

[367] Luther's point here is that, although we on earth can be certain that purgatory leads to heaven, the souls in purgatory do not necessarily share that certainty.

[368] In the *Instructio summaria*, it was claimed that the St Peter's indulgence conferred 'plenaria remissio omnium peccatorum' 'full remission of all sins'; see Leo X's bull *Sacrosanctis salvatoris et redemptoris* (1515), Fabisch/Iserloh, Dokumente, 215, and the *Instructio Summaria*, Fabisch/Iserloh, Dokumente, 264.

24	Falli ob id necesse est maiorem partem populi per indifferentem illam et magnificam pene solute promissionem.	So it necessarily follows that most people are being deceived by the indiscriminate and grandiose promise of punishment being discharged.
25	Qualem potestatem habet papa in purgatorium generaliter, talem habet quilibet Episcopus et Curatus in sua diocesi et parochia specialiter.	The pope has the same power over purgatory in general as any bishop or priest has in his own diocese or parish in particular.
26	Optime facit papa, quod non potestate clavis (quam nullam habet) sed per modum suffragii dat animabus remissionem.	The pope does very well to grant souls remission, not by the power of the keys (which he does not have), but by way of intercession.[369]
27	Hominem predicant, qui statim ut iactus nummus in cistam tinnierit evolare dicunt animam.	Those who say that the soul flies out[370] as soon as the money clinks in the tin are preaching a man-made fiction.[371]
28	Certum est, nummo in cistam tinniente augeri questum et avariciam posse: suffragium autem ecclesie est in arbitrio dei solius.	What is certain is that, when the money clinks in the tin, profit increases, and avarice can too. The church's power of intercession, however, is entirely in God's hands.[372]

[369] Luther refers here to the keys to the kingdom of heaven given by Jesus to St Peter (Matthew 16: 19), which were taken to represent the power given to the clergy to forgive sin. Luther argues that the power of the keys does not extend to purgatory, and that all that the pope can do for souls there is to pray (or 'intercede') on their behalf. Luther's statement here that the pope can actually grant souls remission by intercession is qualified by thesis 28.

[370] i.e. of purgatory.

[371] Luther is referring here to a saying believed to have been used by indulgence preachers.

[372] A papal bull of 3 August 1476 announcing a plenary indulgence mentioned the pope's power to remit the sins of those in purgatory 'per modum suffragii' 'by way of intercession', and the *Instructio summaria* referred to this power; see Fabisch/Iserloh, Dokumente, 269.

29	Quis scit, si omnes anime in purgatorio velint redimi, sicut de s. Severino et Paschali factum narratur.	Who knows whether all the souls in purgatory want to be redeemed, given what is told about St Severinus and St Paschasius?[373]
30	Nullus securus est de veritate sue contritionis, multominus de consecutione plenarie remissionis.	No-one is sure of the truth of their own contrition, let alone of the effectiveness of plenary remission.
31	Quam rarus est vere penitens, tam rarus est vere indulgentias redimens, i.e. rarissimus.	A person actually acquiring remission through indulgences is as rare as someone who is truly penitent, that is, very rare.[374]
32	Damnabuntur ineternum cum suis magistris, qui per literas veniarum securos sese credunt de sua salute.	Those who believe that they have secured their own salvation by indulgence letters will be eternally damned, along with their teachers.
33	Cavendi sunt nimis, qui dicunt venias illas Pape donum esse illud dei inestimabile, quo reconciliatur homo deo.	It is especially important to be on one's guard against those who say that those indulgences of the pope are the inestimable gift of God by which man is reconciled to Him.[375]
34	Gratie enim ille veniales tantum respiciunt penas satisfactionis sacramentalis ab homine constitutas.	For the graces granted by indulgences relate only to the punishments of sacramental satisfaction established by man.

[373] Severinus was archbishop of Cologne in the 4th century and Paschasius (not Paschalius, as Luther spells his name) was deacon of Rome in the 5th century. They were said to have claimed that they would prefer to spend longer in purgatory than necessary, in order to achieve greater glory in heaven.

[374] The Latin literally means, 'A person actually acquiring indulgences … '. In Latin, *indulgentia* can mean both the certificate acquired and the remission to which it entitles the acquirer. Here it refers to the remission.

[375] Luther is referring here to a claim made in the *Instructio summaria*; see Fabisch/Iserloh, Dokumente, 110.

35	Non christiana predicant, qui docent, quod redempturis animas vel confessionalia non sit necessaria contritio.	Those who teach that contrition is unnecessary for those intending to buy souls out of purgatory or to purchase confessional privileges are preaching what is not Christian.[376]
36	Quilibet christianus vere compunctus habet remissionem plenariam a pena et culpa etiam sine literis veniarum sibi debitam.	Any truly remorseful Christian is owed a full remission of punishment and guilt even without letters of indulgence.
37	Quilibet verus christianus, sive vivus sive mortuus, habet participationem omnium bonorum Christi et Ecclesie etiam sine literis veniarum a deo sibi datam.	Any true Christian, whether living or dead, has a God-given share in all the blessings of Christ and the church even without letters of indulgence.[377]
38	Remissio tamen et participatio Pape nullo modo est contemnenda, quia (ut dixi) est declaratio remissionis divine.	Nevertheless, the pope's involvement in remission should in no way be disregarded, for it is, as I have said, a declaration of divine remission.[378]
39	Difficillimum est etiam doctissimis Theologis simul extollere veniarum largitatem et contritionis veritatem coram populo.	It is very difficult even for the most learned theologians to commend to people at one and the same time the bounteousness of indulgences and the truth of contrition.

[376] A confessional privilege allowed the acquirer to choose his or her own confessor. Luther is referring in this thesis to two claims made in the *Instructio summaria*; see Fabisch/Iserloh, Dokumente, 267, 269.

[377] The phrase *participatio omnium bonorum ecclesiae* 'a share in all the blessings of the church' was an established term for various spiritual blessings to which Christians were entitled, and is mentioned in the *Instructio summaria* as one of the benefits of indulgences; see Fabisch/Iserloh, Dokumente, 268–69.

[378] This thesis repeats the argument in thesis 6 that the pope has the power to declare God's remission (even if not to grant remission himself).

40	Contritionis veritas penas querit et amat, Veniarum autem largitas relaxat et odisse facit, saltem occasione.	True contrition seeks out and craves punishments, but bounteous indulgences release people from punishments and make people hate them, or at least give them the opportunity to do so.
41	Caute sunt venie apostolice predicande, ne populus false intelligat eas preferri ceteris bonis operibus charitatis.	Apostolic indulgences should be preached with caution, in case people erroneously think that they are preferable to other good works of love.[379]
42	Docendi sunt christiani, quod Pape mens non est, redemptionem veniarum ulla ex parte comparandam esse operibus misericordie.	Christians should be taught that the pope does not mean the buying of indulgences to be at all comparable with merciful works.
43	Docendi sunt christiani, quod dans pauperi aut mutuans egenti melius facit quam si venias redimeret.	Christians should be taught that giving to the poor or lending to the needy is better than buying indulgences.[380]
44	Quia per opus charitatis crescit charitas et fit homo melior, sed per venias non fit melior sed tantummodo a pena liberior.	For love grows and people are made better by works of love, but they do not become better by indulgences, only freer from punishment.
45	Docendi sunt christiani, quod, qui videt egenum et neglecto eo dat pro veniis, non indulgentias Pape sed indignationem dei sibi vendicat.	Christians should be taught that anyone who sees a needy person, passes him by, and spends money on indulgences is not buying the pope's indulgences but God's wrath.
46	Docendi sunt christiani, quod nisi superfluis abundent	Christians should be taught that, unless they have more than

[379] Apostolic indulgences were those granted by the pope (as successor to the apostle St Peter). The St Peter's indulgence (see Introduction, p. xxii) was one such. The relationship between indulgences and good works is the subject of *Sermon* 16.

[380] See Matthew 5: 42.

	necessaria tenentur domui sue retinere et nequaquam propter venias effundere.	enough, they are required to keep what is necessary for their household and on no account squander it on indulgences.[381]
47	Docendi sunt christiani, quod redemptio veniarum est libera, non precepta.	Christians should be taught that buying indulgences is a choice, not a command.[382]
48	Docendi sunt christiani, quod Papa sicut magis eget ita magis optat in veniis dandis pro se devotam orationem quam promptam pecuniam.	Christians should be taught that the pope, in granting indulgences, needs and therefore desires their devout prayer more than their ready money.
49	Docendi sunt christiani, quod venie Pape sunt utiles, si non in eas confidant, Sed nocentissime, si timorem dei per eas amittant.	Christians should be taught that papal indulgences are useful if people do not put their trust in them, but extremely harmful if they lose their fear of God because of them.
50	Docendi sunt christiani, quod, si Papa nosset exactiones venialium predicatorum, mallet Basilicam s. Petri in cineres ire quam edificari cute, carne et ossibus ovium suarum.	Christians should be taught that, if the pope knew about the exactions of indulgence preachers, he would sooner see St Peter's Basilica reduced to ashes than built from the skin, flesh, and bones of his flock.[383]
51	Docendi sunt christiani, quod Papa sicut debet ita vellet, etiam vendita (si opus sit) Basilica s. Petri, de suis pecuniis dare illis, a quorum plurimis quidam concionatores veniarum pecuniam eliciunt.	Christians should be taught that the pope would, as he must, be willing to give some of his own money to the many who have been swindled by certain hawkers of indulgences – even selling St Peter's Basilica if necessary.

381 See *Sermon* 16.

382 See *Sermon* 17.

383 St Peter's Basilica in Rome was to be funded by the proceeds of the sale of indulgences (see Introduction, p. xxii).

52	Vana est fiducia salutis per literas veniarum, etiam si Commissarius, immo Papa ipse suam animam pro illis impigneraret.	It is pointless to rely on letters of indulgence for salvation, even if the indulgence commissioner, or for that matter the pope himself, offered his own soul as security for them.[384]
53	Hostes Christi et Pape sunt ii, qui propter venias predicandas verbum dei in aliis ecclesiis penitus silere iubent.	Those who order the word of God to be completely silenced in other churches so that indulgences may be preached are the enemies of Christ and the pope.[385]
54	Iniuria fit verbo dei, dum in eodem sermone equale vel longius tempus impenditur veniis quam illi.	It is offensive to the word of God when, in the same sermon, as much or more time is devoted to indulgences as to God's word.
55	Mens Pape necessario est, quod, si venie (quod minimum est) una campana, unis pompis et ceremoniis celebrantur, Euangelium (quod maximum est) centum campanis, centum pompis, centum ceremoniis predicetur.	The pope's attitude must be that, if indulgences (which are the most insignificant thing) are celebrated by one bell, one procession, and one ceremony, the gospel (which is the greatest thing) should be preached with a hundred bells, a hundred processions, a hundred ceremonies.[386]
56	Thesauri ecclesie, unde Papa dat iudulgentias, neque satis nominati sunt neque cogniti apud populum Christi.	The treasures of the church, out of which the pope grants indulgences, are neither sufficiently mentioned nor known about among the people of Christ.[387]

[384] The indulgence commissioner was the most senior official responsible for the preaching of indulgences.

[385] This requirement appears in the *Instructio summaria*; see Fabisch/Iserloh, Dokumente, 261.

[386] Johann Tetzel's preaching of indulgences was accompanied by elaborate ceremony.

[387] The 'treasures of the church' or 'treasury of merits' refers to the store of good works built up by Christ and the saints from which the pope could draw the indulgences he granted; see Introduction, pp. xviii–xix.

57	Temporales certe non esse patet, quod non tam facile eos profundunt, sed tantummodo colligunt multi concionatorum.	It is very clear that these are not worldly treasures, because many hawkers of indulgences do not so much give away such treasures willingly, but just collect them.[388]
58	Nec sunt merita Christi et sanctorum, quia hec semper sine Papa operantur gratiam hominis interioris et crucem, mortem infernumque exterioris.	Nor are they the merits of Christ and the saints, for these merits – always without the pope – bring about grace in the inner person and the cross, death, and hell in the outer person.
59	Thesauros ecclesie s. Laurentius dixit esse pauperes ecclesie, sed locutus est usu vocabuli suo tempore.	St Lawrence said that the poor of the church were her treasures, but he was using the word in the sense that it had in his own time.[389]
60	Sine temeritate dicimus claves ecclesie (merito Christi donatas) esse thesaurum istum.	It is not lightly that we call the keys of the church (given by the merit of Christ) that treasure.
61	Clarum est enim, quod ad remissionem penarum et casuum sola sufficit potestas Pape.	For it is clear that the pope's power on its own is sufficient for the remission of punishments and legal actions.[390]
62	Verus thesaurus ecclesie est sacrosanctum euangelium glorie et gratie dei.	The true treasure of the church is the most sacred gospel of God's glory and grace.

[388] Luther's point is that the treasures of the church obviously do not have any worldly (or material) value, because indulgence preachers would not willingly give anything of worldly value away.

[389] St Lawrence was archdeacon of Rome in the 3rd century. Before being put to death by the Roman authorities, he was ordered to hand over all the church's wealth. He quickly distributed it to the poor, and is then reported to have used the words referred to here by Luther.

[390] The punishments here are the penalties imposed by the church (see thesis 5); legal actions are those decided by the papal curia as the highest church court.

63	Hic autem est merito odiosissimus, quia ex primis facit novissimos.	But this treasure is naturally most detestable, since it causes the first to be last.[391]
64	Thesaurus autem indulgentiarum merito est gratissimus, quia ex novissimis facit primos.	By contrast the treasure of indulgences is naturally most acceptable, since it causes the last to be first.
65	Igitur thesauri Euangelici rhetia sunt, quibus olim piscabantur viros divitiarum.	Therefore the treasures of the gospel are the nets with which they once fished for men of wealth.[392]
66	Thesauri indulgentiarum rhetia sunt, quibus nunc piscantur divitias virorum.	The treasures of indulgences are the nets with which they[393] now fish for the wealth of men.
67	Indulgentie, quas concionatores vociferantur maximas gratias, intelliguntur vere tales quoad questum promovendum.	The benefits of indulgences, which the hawkers hail as being greater than all others, can indeed be understood as such – insofar as they promote gain.[394]
68	Sunt tamen re vera minime ad gratiam dei et crucis pietatem comparate.	Yet they are, in fact, most insignificant compared with the grace of God and the mercifulness of the cross.
69	Tenentur Episcopi et Curati veniarum apostolicarum Commissarios cum omni reverentia admittere.	Bishops and priests are obliged to receive the commissioners of apostolic indulgences with all reverence.
70	Sed magis tenentur omnibus oculis intendere, omnibus auribus advertere, ne pro	But more than this they are obliged to be all eyes and all ears in case those men preach their

[391] In this and the next thesis Luther is echoing Matthew 19: 30 and 20: 16.

[392] This thesis and the next allude to Matthew 4: 19.

[393] 'they' are presumably indulgence preachers.

[394] Luther makes a play on the word Latin *gratia* which can mean 'recompense, benefit', as well as 'grace'. The *Instructio summaria* listed the different prices of an indulgence to be charged according to the purchaser's station in life. See Fabisch/Iserloh, Dokumente, 265–67.

	commissione Pape sua illi somnia predicent.	own fantasies instead of what the pope has commissioned.
71	Contra veniarum apostolicarum veritatem qui loquitur, sit ille anathema et maledictus.	Let anyone who denies the truth about apostolic indulgences be excommunicated and cursed.
72	Qui vero contra libidinem ac licentiam verborum Concionatoris veniarum curam agit, sit ille benedictus.	But let anyone who is concerned about the greedy and unrestrained words of indulgence hawkers be blessed.
73	Sicut Papa iuste fulminat eos, qui in fraudem negocii veniarum quacunque arte machinantur,	Just as the pope justly thunders against those who contrive harm in any way to the trade in indulgences,[395]
74	Multomagis fulminare intendit eos, qui per veniarum pretextum in fraudem sancte charitatis et veritatis machinantur.	so much more does he intend to thunder against those who use indulgences as a pretext to contrive harm to holy love and truth.
75	Opinari venias papales tantas esse, ut solvere possint hominem, etiam si quis per impossibile dei genitricem violasset, Est insanire.	To think that papal indulgences are so great that they could absolve someone even if they had done the impossible and violated the mother of God is madness.[396]
76	Dicimus contra, quod venie papales nec minimum venialium peccatorum tollere possint quo ad culpam.	On the contrary, we say that papal indulgences cannot remove even the most minor of venial sins as far as guilt is concerned.[397]
77	Quod dicitur, nec si s. Petrus modo Papa esset maiores gratias donare posset, est	To say that even St Peter, if he were pope, could not bestow graces greater than these is

[395] The *Instructio summaria* threatened to punish anyone impeding the preaching of indulgences; see Fabisch/Iserloh, Dokumente, 258–59.

[396] Luther attributed the claim made in this thesis to Johann Tetzel, who denied it. Luther also attributed the claims in theses 77 and 79 to Tetzel.

[397] See thesis 6. Venial sins were minor sins punishable with small penalties; they contrasted with mortal sins which, if not absolved before death, made the sinner liable to punishment in hell.

	blasphemia in sanctum Petrum et Papam.	blasphemy against St Peter and the pope.
78	Dicimus contra, quod etiam iste et quilibet papa maiores habet, scilicet Euangelium, virtutes, gratias curationum &c. ut 1. Co. xij.	On the contrary, we say that even he – and any pope – possesses graces which are greater, namely the gospel, miracles, gifts of healing, etc., as it says in 1 Corinthians 12: 28.
79	Dicere, Crucem armis papalibus insigniter erectam cruci Christi equivalere, blasphemia est.	To say that a cross emblazoned with the papal coat of arms is equivalent to the cross of Christ is blasphemy.[398]
80	Rationem reddent Episcopi, Curati et Theologi, Qui tales sermones in populum licere sinunt.	Bishops, priests, and theologians who give free rein to such talk among the people will be held to account for this.
81	Facit hec licentiosa veniarum predicatio, ut nec reverentiam Pape facile sit etiam doctis viris redimere a calumniis aut certe argutis questionibus laicorum.	This arbitrary preaching of indulgences makes it difficult even for learned men to rescue the dignity of the pope from slander or at any rate from the perceptive questions of lay people.
82	Scilicet. Cur Papa non evacuat purgatorium propter sanctissimam charitatem et summam animarum necessitatem ut causam omnium iustissimam, Si infinitas animas redimit propter pecuniam funestissimam ad structuram Basilice ut causam levissimam?	For example: 'Why does the pope not empty purgatory for the sake of the most sacred love and the extreme distress suffered by souls there (which is the most just reason of all to do so), if he redeems an infinite number of souls for the sake of the wretched money it takes to build a church (which is the most trivial reason to do so)?'
83	Item. Cur permanent exequie et anniversaria defunctorum et non reddit aut recipi permittit	Or: 'Why are funeral and anniversary masses still held for the dead and why does he not give

[398] Luther is referring to the ceremonial procession which accompanied the preaching of indulgences.

	beneficia pro illis instituta, cum iam sit iniuria pro redemptis orare?	back or allow the return of the endowments set up for them, since it is now wrong to pray for the redeemed?'[399]
84	Item. Que illa nova pietas Dei et Pape, quod impio et inimico propter pecuniam concedunt animam piam et amicam dei redimere, Et tamen propter necessitatem ipsius met pie et dilecte anime non redimunt eam gratuita charitate?	Or: 'What is this new piety of God and the pope, that they allow an impious man who is their enemy to redeem for money a pious soul who is friendly to God, and yet they do not, given the distress of that pious and beloved soul, redeem it purely out of love?'[400]
85	Item. Cur Canones penitentiales re ipsa et non usu iam diu in semet abrogati et mortui adhuc tamen pecuniis redimuntur per concessionem indulgentiarum tanquam vivacissimi?	Or: 'Why are the penitential canons – themselves long since abrogated and dead in fact and not by use[401] – still being bought off for money through the granting of indulgences as if they were still very much alive?'
86	Item. Cur Papa, cuius opes hodie sunt opulentissimis Crassis crassiores, non de suis pecuniis magis quam pauperum fidelium struit unam tantummodo Basilicam sancti Petri?	Or: 'Why does the pope, who is rich enough today to out-Crassus Crassus, not build this one single Basilica of St Peter with his own money rather than that of the faithful poor ?'[402]

---

399 Anniversary masses were held on the anniversary of a person's death. Canon law did not allow prayers to be said for saints (who were already in heaven) or the damned (who were in hell).

400 Luther may be referring here to a part of the *Instructio summaria* which stated that those buying indulgences for souls in purgatory did not themselves have to be contrite; see Fabisch/Iserloh, Dokumente, 269.

401 The *Resolutiones* (see Introduction, p. xi) do not comment on this thesis, which has been read in different ways. Luther appears to be reflecting a popular concern that penitential canons have had no theoretical or practical relevance for a long time, in which case 'not by use' means 'not just because of a lack of use'.

402 In the Latin there is a pun on the name of Crassus, the wealthy Roman general (115–53 B.C.), and *crassus* meaning 'fat'.

87	Item. Quid remittit aut participat Papa iis, qui per contritionem perfectam ius habent plenarie remissionis et participationis?	Or: 'What is it that the pope grants as remission or participation to those who, by perfect contrition, have a right to full remission and participation?'
88	Item. Quid adderetur ecclesie boni maioris, Si Papa, sicut semel facit, ita centies in die cuilibet fidelium has remissiones et participationes tribueret?	Or: 'What greater good could come to the church than if the pope were to bestow these remissions and participations a hundred time a day to each of the faithful rather than once, as he does now?'[403]
89	Ex quo Papa salutem querit animarum per venias magis quam pecunias, Cur suspendit literas et venias iam olim concessas, cum sint eque efficaces?	'Since the pope seeks the salvation of souls rather than money through indulgences, why does he suspend letters and indulgences previously granted, even though they are equally effective?'[404]
90	Hec scrupulosissima laicorum argumenta sola potestate compescere nec reddita ratione diluere, Est ecclesiam et Papam hostibus ridendos exponere et infelices christianos facere.	To suppress these very penetrating arguments of the laity by force alone and not to dispel them by giving reasons exposes the church and the pope to the ridicule of their enemies and makes the life of Christians a misery.
91	Si ergo venie secundum spiritum et mentem Pape predicarentur, facile illa omnia solverentur, immo non essent.	If, therefore, indulgences were preached according to the spirit and intention of the pope, all of these matters would be easily

[403]As mentioned in the *Instructio summaria*, a plenary indulgence allowed its owner to receive absolution once in their lifetime and once just before death; see Fabisch/Iserloh, Dokumente, 267.

[404] Pope Leo X did precisely this in the bull of 31 March 1515 proclaiming the St Peter's Indulgence.

		resolved – in fact, they would not arise.[405]
92	Valeant itaque omnes illi prophete, qui dicunt populo Christi 'Pax pax', et non est pax.	Away, then, with all those prophets who say to the people of Christ, 'Peace, peace', and there is no peace.[406]
93	Bene agant omnes illi prophete, qui dicunt populo Christi 'Crux crux', et non est crux.	Blessed be all those prophets who say to the people of Christ, 'Cross, cross', and there is no cross.
94	Exhortandi sunt Christiani, ut caput suum Christum per penas, mortes infernosque sequi studeant,	Christians should be encouraged eagerly to follow Christ their head through punishment, death, and hell,[407]
95	Ac sic magis per multas tribulationes intrare celum quam per securitatem pacis confidant.	and in this way to be confident of entering heaven through many tribulations rather than through the complacency of peace.[408]
	M.D.Xvij.	1517

[405] Luther's point is that if his earlier arguments about the limits of papal remission were followed (e.g. thesis 5), the objections in Theses 82–89 would not come up.
[406] An allusion to Jeremiah 6: 14 and 8: 11 and Ezekiel 13: 10, 16. In this thesis and the next Luther argues that an acceptance of turmoil and punishment leads to their elimination.
[407] The idea of Christ as the head can be found in Ephesians 1: 22; 4: 15; 5: 23; and Colossians 1: 18.
[408] An allusion to Acts 14: 22.

Facsimiles of the *Sermon von Ablass und Gnade*

Basel: Pamphilus Gengenbach 1518	F2,4,6,8,10,12,14,16
Leipzig: Valentin Schumann 1518	F3,5,7,9,11,13,15, 17

The facsimiles are arranged on facing pages with the Basel edition on the left and the Leipzig edition on the right to allow a page-by-page comparison of the text, layout, and annotation of the two Taylorian copies; the format is slightly reduced to fit the page width. Actual-size facsimiles in full colour can be downloaded from the website editions.mml.ox.ac.uk.

The borders on this page are from the title-page of the Leipzig copy (above) and the Basel copy (below).

EJn Sermon oder Predig
von dem ablasz vnd gnade
durch den wirdigen docto-
rem Martinum Luther Augu
stiner zu wittenbergk ge-
macht vnd gepre
diget.

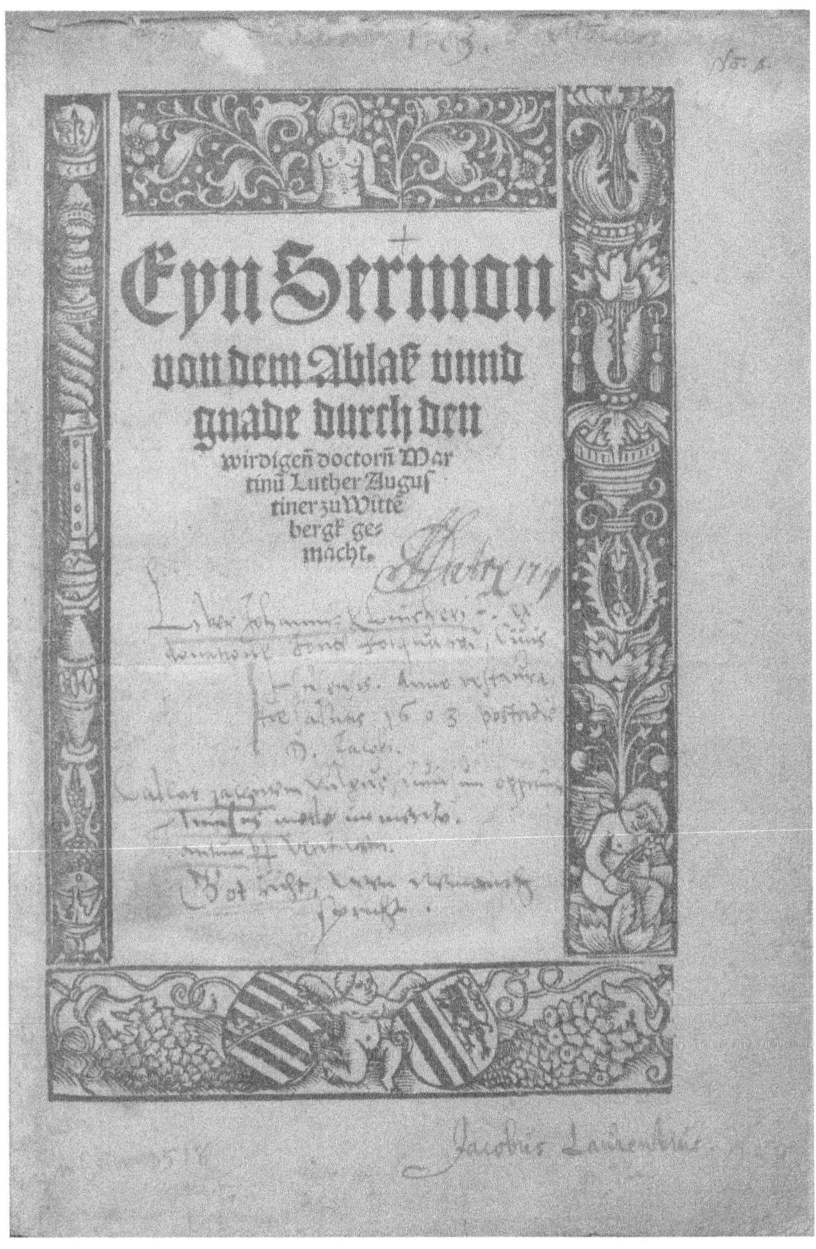

Eyn Sermon
von dem Ablaß unnd
gnade durch den
wirdigeñ doctorñ Mar
tinũ Luther August
tiner zu Witte
bergk ge
macht.

Ein Sermon oder Predig võ dem ab
laſz vnd gnade durch den wirdigen do
ctorem Martinum Luther Auguſti/
ner zu wittenbergk gemacht vnd ge/
prediget.

Zů dem erſten ſöllend jr wiſſen/das etzlich
new lerer/als Magiſter Sen. S. Tomas
vnd jre volger geben der bůſz drey theil.
Nemlich die rew/die beicht/die gnůgthů/
ung/vnd wie wol diſer vnderſcheid nach
jrer meinung/ſchwerlich oder auch gar ni
chts/gegründet erfunden wirt yn der heiligẽ geſchrifft/no
ch yn den alten heiligen Chriſtelichen lerern/doch wellẽd
wir das jetzund alſo laſſen belibẽ/vnd nach jrer wyſz redẽ.

¶ Zů dem andern ſagen ſie/der ablaſz nympt nicht hyn/dz
erſt oder ander theil. Das iſt die rew oder beycht/ſunder dz
dritt. Nemlich die gnůgthůung.

¶ Zů dem dritten. Die gnůg thůung wirt weiter geteilet/jn
drey theil. Das iſt Bätten/vaſten/almůſen. Alſo das bättẽ
begreiff allerley wärck der ſelen eygen. Als läſen/tychten/
hören gottes wort/predigen leren vnd der gleichen. Vaſtẽ
begreiff allerley wärck der caſteyung ſeins flaiſchs als wa
chen/arbeiten/hart ligẽ/cleyder ꝛc. Almůſen begreiff aller/
ley gůte wärck der lieb vnd barmhärtzigkeit gegen dẽ nä/
chſten.

¶ Zů dem vierden/ Jſt by yn allen vngezweifflet/das der
ablaſz hynnympt dieſelbẽ wärck der gnůgthůung/für die

Eyn Sermon von dem Ablaß vnnd gnade/ durch den wirdigen doctorn Martinum Luther Augustiner zu Wittenbergk geprediget.

¶ Czum Ersten solt yr wissen/ das eczlich new lerer/ als Magister Sentē. S. Thomas vñ yhre folger gebē d̕ pusz drey teyl/ Nemlich die rew/ die peycht/ die gnugthuung/ Vñ wiewol diszer vnderscheyd nach yrer meynung/ schwerlich adder auch gar nichts/ gegrundet erfunden wirt in der heyligenn schrifft/ noch in den alten heyligen Christlichen lererñ/ doch wollē wir das yczt szo lassen bleyben/ vnd nach yrher weysz reden.

¶ Czum andernñ sagen sie/ der ablasz nympt nycht hynn das erst adder ander teyll/ das ist/ die rew adder peycht/ sunderñ das dritt/ nemlich die gnugthuung.

¶ Czum Driten. die gnugthuung wirt weyter geteylet in drey teil/ das ist/ Beeten/ vastē/ almuszē/ also/ das beetē begreyfft allerlei werck der seelē eygē/ als leszē/ tichten/ horen gottes wort/ predigen/ leeren vnd d̕ gleichen. Vasten begreiff allerlei werck der casteyūg seins fleyschs/ als wachen/ erbeiten/ hart lager/ cleider ꝛc. Almuszē begreyff allerlei gute werck der lyeb vñ barmherczickeyt gegen dem nehsten.

¶ Czum Vierden/ Ist bey yhn allē vngeczweyfelt/ das der ablas hin nympt die selben werck der gnugthuūg/ vor die sund schuldig czuthun adder auffgeseczt/ dann szo er die selben werck solt all hin nehmen/ blieb nichts gutes mehr da/ das wir thun mochtenn.

ſünd ſchuldig zů thůn oder vffgeſetzt/dañ ſo er die ſelben
wårck ſolt all hyn nåmen/blyb nichts gůtes meer da/das
wir thůn möchten.

¶Zů dem fünfften. Jſt by vylen geweſt ein groſſe vnd no-
ch vnbeſchloſzne opiny/ob d̕ ablaſz auch etwas meer hyn-
nåme dañ ſolche vffgelegte gůte wårck. Nemlich ob er au-
ch die pyne/die die göttlich gerechtigkeit für die ſünde for-
dert/abneme.

¶Zů dem ſächſten. Laſz ich yre opiny vnuerworffen auff
diſz mal. Das ſag ich/das man auſz keiner geſchryfft bewe-
ren kan/das göttlich gerechtigkeit etwas pyn oder gnůg-
thůung begerē oder fordere von dem ſünder. Dañ allein ſy
ne hårtzliche vnd ware rew oder bekerūg mit fürſatz hyn-
fürter das Crütz chriſti zů tragen/vnd die obgenātē wårck
(auch von niemandt auff geſetzt) zů üben. Dañ alſo ſpricht
er durch Ezechiā. wañ ſich der ſünder bekert/vnd thůt re/
cht/ſo wil ich ſeiner ſünd nit meer gedenckē. Jtem alſo hat
er ſelbs all die abſoluiert. Mariā magda. den gichtpruchi-
gen/die eebråcherynn ꝛc. Und möcht wol gern hören wår
das anders bewåren ſoll. Unangeſehen das etliche docto
res alſo gedaucht hat.

¶Zů dem ſybēdē. Das findet man wol/das got ettlich na
ch ſiner gerechtigkeit ſtraffet/oder durch pein dringt zů der
rew. wie jm̄ Pſal. 88. So ſein kinder werden ſünden/ will
ich mit der rütē jre ſünd heimſůchē/Aber doch mein barm-
hårtzigkeit nit von yn wenden. Aber dyſe pein ſtot yn nie-
mandts gewalt nach zů laſſen/dañ allein gottes. Ja er wil
ſie nit laſſen/ſunder verſpricht/er wöll ſie aufflegen.

¶Zů dē achtē. Der halbē ſo kan man der ſelben gedückten
pein keinē namē geben/weiſz auch niemandt/was ſie jſt/ſo
ſie diſe ſtraff nit jſt/auch die gůten obgenantē wårck nit jſt.

¶ Czum Funfften. Ist bey vielẽ gewest eyn grosse vñ noch vnbeschlosszene opiny / Ab der ablas auch etwas mehr hynnehme / dann solche auffgelegte gute werck / nemlich / ab er auch die peyne / die die gotlich gerechtigkeyt / vor die sunde / fordert / abnehme.

¶ Czum Sechsten. Lasz ich yhre opiny vnuorworffen auff das mal / Das sag ich / das mã ausz keyner schrifft beweren kañ / das gottlich gerechtigkeyt etwas peyn adder gnugthuung begere adder fordere / vonn dem sunder. Dañ allein seyne herczliche vnd ware rew adder bekerũg myt vorsacz hynfurder / das Creucz Christi czu tragenn / vnnd die obgenanten werck (auch von nyemãt auffgesetzt) czu vben / Dañ szo spricht er durch Ezechie. Wan sich der sunder bekeret / vñ thut recht / so will ich seyner sunde nicht mehr gedencken. Item also hatt er selbs all die absoluirt. Maria Magda. den gichtpruchtigẽ. Die eebrecherynne ꝛc. Und mocht woll gerne horen wer das anders bewerẽ soll. Unangesehen das eczlich doctores szo gedaucht haben.

¶ Czum Sibenden. Das findet man woll / das gott eczlich nach seyner gerechtigkeyt straffet / Aber durch peyne dringt czu der rew / wie ym. 88. ps. Szo seyn kinder werden sundigen / will ich myt der ruthen / yhre sunde heym suchen / Aber doch meyn barmherczickeyt nit von yhnn wendẽ. Aber disze peyne / stehet in nyemandes gewalt nachczulassen / dann alleyne gottis. Ja er will sie nit lassen / sunder vorspricht / er woll sie auflegẽ.

¶ Czum Achten. Der halbẽ szo kann man der selbẽ gedunckten peyn / keynen namen geben / weysz auch nyemant / was sye ist / szo sie disze straff nyt ist. auch dye guten obgenanten werck nit ist.

¶Zů dē nündē sag ich/ob die Christēlich kirch noch heüt
beschlusz vnd ausz erkleret/dz der ablasz meer dañ die wer
cke der gnůgthůung hyn nāme/so were dannocht tausent
mal besser/das kein christen mensch dē ablasz löset oder be
geret/sunder das sie lieber die werck thäten vnd die pein
littē. Dañ der ablasz neüt anders ist/noch anders mag wer
den/dañ nachlassung gůter wärck vnd heilsamer pein/die
man doch billicher solt erwelen dañ verlassen. Wie wol et
lich der newen prediger zweierley pein erfundē. Medica-
tiuas. Satisfactorias. Das ist etzlich pein zů der gnůgthů-
ung/etzliche zů der besserūg. Aber wir haben meer frybeit
zů verachten (got zů lob) solichs vnd des gleichen plaude
ry/dañ sie habē zů ertichtē/dañ alle pein/Ja alles was got
vfflegt/ist besserlich vnd zůträglicher den christen.

¶Zů dem zehenden/das ist nichts geredt/das der pein vñ
wärck zů vyl syen/ das der mensch sie nit mög volbringen
der kürtze halben seines läbens/darumb dañ inen not sey
der Ablasz. Antwort ich/Dz das kein grund hab vnd ein
lauter gedicht ist. Dañ gott vnd die heilig kirche legen nie
mandt mee auff dañ yn zů tragen müglich ist. Als dañ au
ch sant Paulus sagt. Das got nit lasz versůcht werden je-
mādt meer dañ er tragē mag/ vnd es lāget nit wenig zů
der christenheit schmach/dz man ir schuld gibt/sie lege auff
meer dañ wir tragen mögen.

¶Zů dem elfften. Wañ gleich die bůsz im geystlichen rech-
ten gesetzt/jtzet nach gingen. Das für ein jegliche totsünd
syben jar bůsz vffgelegt were/So můst doch die Christen-
heit die selben gesetz lassen/vnd nit weiter aufflegen/dañ sy
einē jetlichen zů tragen weren. Vyl weniger/so sie nun je-
tzund nicht sind/so soll man achtē/das meer vffgelegt wer
de dañ jederman wol ertragen kan.

¶Zů dem zwölfften. Man sagt wol/dz der sünder mit der

¶ Czum Neunden. Sag ich/ ob die Chriſtenliche kirch noch heut beſchluſz/ vnd auſz erclerer/ das der ablas mehr dañ die werck der gnugthuũg hyn neme/ ſzo were es den nocht tauſentmal beſſer/ das keyn Chriſten menſch den ablas loſzet oder begeret/ ſunderñ das ſye lieber die werck thetten vnnd die peyn litten/ dañ der ablas/ nit anderſt iſt nach mag werden/ dañ nachlaſſung gutter werck/ vnnd heylſamer peyn/ die man billich ſolt erwellẽ dañ vorlaſſen/ wiewol etlich d' newen prediger zweyerley peyne erfunden/ Medicatiuas Satiſfactorias/ das iſt etzlich peyn czur gnugthuung/ eczlich czur beſſerung/ Aber wir haben mehr freyheyt czuuorachten (got lob) ſulchs vnnd des gleychen plauderey/ dañ ſie haben czu ertichten/ dañ alle peyn/ ya alls was gott auff legt/ iſt beſſerlich vnd tzu treglich den Chriſten.

¶ Czũ czehenden/ Das iſt nichts geredt/ das der peyn vnnd werck czu vill ſeynn/ das der menſch ſye nit mag volbrengen/ der kurcz halben ſeyns lebens/ Darumb yhm nott ſey der Ablas. Antwort ich das/ das keyn grundt hab/ vñ eyn lauter getichtiſt/ Dañ gott vnnd die heylige kirche/ legen nyemand mehr auff/ dañ yhm czu tragẽ muglich iſt/ als auch. S. Paul ſagt/ das got nit leſzt vorſucht werden yemand/ mehr dañ er mag tragen/ vnd es langet nit wenig czu der Chriſtenheyt ſchmach/ Das mã yhr ſchuld gibt/ ſye lege auff mehr/ dañ wir tragen kunen.

¶ Czum eylfften. Wann gleych die puſz ym geyſtlichẽ recht geſeczt/ iczt noch ginge/ Das vor ein yglich todtſund/ ſyeben iar puſz auffgelegt were/ Szo muſt doch die Chriſtenheyt/ dye ſelbẽ geſecz laſſen/ vñ nit weyter auff legen/ dañ ſye eynem yglichen czu tragẽ warẽ. Vil weniger/ nu ſye iczt nicht ſeyn/ ſall mã achtẽ/ das nicht mehr auffgelegt werde dañ yederman wol tragẽ kan.

vberingen peyn jns fägfewr/ader zum ablasz geweiset soll
werden/aber es wirt wol meer dings on allen grund vnd
bewerung gesagt.

¶Zů dē dryzehendē. Es jst ein grosser jrthum das jemādt
meine er wölle gnůg thůn für seine sünd/so doch got die sel
ben alle zeit vmb sunst ausz vnschetzlicher gnad verzyhet/
nicht dar für begerend/dañ hynfürter wol leben. Die Chri
stenheit fordert wol etwas/also mag sy vnd soll auch das
selb nachlassen/vnd nichts schwerers oder vnträglichers
vfflegen.

¶Zů dem vierzehenden. Ablasz wirt zů gelassen vmb der
vnuolkōnen vnd faulen christen willen/die sich nit wöllē
kåcklich üben yn gůten werckē/oder vnleidlich sind. Dañ
ablasz fürdert niemandt zum bessern/sunder duldet vñ zů-
laszt jr vnuolkōmenheit. Darumb soll man nit wider den
ablasz reden/man soll aber auch niemandt dar zů reden.

¶Zů dē fünffzehenden. Vyl sicherer vnd besserer thet der/
der luter vmb gottes willē/gebe zů dē gebew sant Peters
oder was sunst genāt wirt/ Dañ das er ablasz dar für nå-
me/dañ es ferlich jst/das er solch gabe vmb desz ablasz wil
len vnd nit vmb gottes willen gybt.

¶Zů dem såchzehendē. Vyl besser jst das wårck einē dürff
tigen erzeigt/dañ das zů dem gebew geben/auch vyl bes-
ser dañ der ablasz dar für geben (dañ wie gesagt) Es jst bes
ser ein gůtes werck gethan/dañ vyl nach gelassen. Ablasz
aber/jst nachlassung vyl gůter wårck/ oder jst nichts nach
gelassen.

¶Aber das jch eüch recht vnderwyse/so merckt vff. Du
solt vor allen dingē (weder sant Peters gebewd/noch ab
las angesehen) deinē nåchstē armen gebē/wiltu etwas ge-
ben. Wañ es aber dabyn küpt/das niemandt yn diner stat

¶ Czum czwelfftē. Man ſagt wol / das der ſunder mit der vberingen peyn/ inſzfegfewr oder czum ablas geweyſet ſall werdenn/ aber es wirt wol mehr dings/ an grundt vnd beweruug geſagt.

¶ Czum Dreyczehendē. Es iſt eyn groſzer yrthū das yemādt meyne /er wolle gnugthun vor ſeyne ſundt/ ſo doch got die ſelbē alczeyt vmb ſunſt/ auſz vnſcheczlich er gnad vorczeyhet/ nichts darfur begerend dā hynfur der woll leben. Die Chriſtenheyt fordert wol etwas/ alſo mag ſie vnd ſall auch das ſelb nachlaſſen / vnnd nichts ſchweres adder vntreglichs auf legen.

¶ Czum Uierczehendē. Ablaſz wirt czu gelaſſen vmb der vnuolkōmen vnd faulen Chriſten willen / die ſich nit wollen kecklich vben in guten wercken/ oder vnleydlich ſeyn / dañ ablas furdert nyeman czum beſſern/ ſundern duldet vnnd zuleſzet yr vnuolkōmen/ darumb ſoll man nit wider das ablas redenn / man ſall aber auch nyemand darczu reden.

¶ Czum Funffczehenden. Uill ſicherer/ vnnd beſſerer thet der/ der lauter vmb gottes willen/ gebe czu dē gebewde. S. Petri/ ader was ſunſt genāt wirt/ Dan das er ablas darfur nehme/ dann es ferlich iſt/ das er ſulch gabe vmb des ablas willē vñ nit vmb gotts willē gibt

¶ Czum Sechczehendē. Uill beſſer iſt das werck eynen durfftigen erczeygt/ dan das czum gebewde geben wirt auch vill beſſer/ dan der ablas dafur gegebē/ dan wie geſagt. Es iſt beſſer eyn gutes werck gethā/ dann vill nach gelaſſen. Ablas aber/ iſt nachlaſſung villguter werck/ ader iſt nichts nach gelaſſen.

A iij

ist der hilff bedarff (das ob got will niemer geschehen soll) dañ soltu gebē so du wilt zů den kirchē/altarn/geschmuck/kelich/die yn deiner stat sind. Und wañ das auch nun nit meer not ist. Dañ aller erst/so du wilt/magstu gebem zů dē gebēwde sant Peters oder anderswo. Auch saltu dannocht nit das umb ablasz willē thůn. Dañ sant Paulus spricht. wer seinē hausz genossen nit wol thůt/ist kein Christen vnd erger dañ ein haide/Und halts dar für fry/wer dir anders sagt der verfůrt dich/vnd sůcht dein seel in deinē Bůtell/vnd fund er pfennig darinne/dz wär jm lieber dañ all selen. So sprichst du. So würd ich niemer me ablasz lösen. Antwort ich/Das hab ich schon oben gesagt. Das mein will/begirde/bitt vñ rot ist/das niemād ablasz löse/lasz die faulen schläfferigen ablasz lösen/gang du für dich.

¶ Zů dem sibenzehendē. Der ablasz ist nit gebottē/auch nit geratē/sunder vō der dinger zal/die zů gelassen vñ erloubt werden/darumb ist es nit ein wärck desz gehorsams/auch nit verdienstlich/sunder ein vszug desz gehorsams. Darūb wie wol man niemādt werē soll den ablasz zů lösen/so soll man doch alle christen dar von ziehen/vnd zů den werckē vnd peynen/die do nach gelassen reitzen vnd stercken.

¶ Zů dem achtzehenden. Ob die seelen ausz dem fägfewr gezogen werden durch dē ablasz/weisz ich nit/vnd geloub das auch noch nicht/wie wol dz etzliche newe doctores sagen/ist ynē aber vnmüglich zů bewerē/auch hat es die kirch noch nit beschlossen/darumb zů merer sicherheit ist besser das du für sie selbs bittest vnd würckest/dañ disz ist bewerter vnd ist gewisz.

¶ Zů dē neünzehenden. In disen puncten hab ich nit zwyfel/vnd sind gnůgsam in der geschryfft gegründt. Darumb solt jr auch kein zwyfel haben/vnd last doctores/scholasticos/scholasticos sein/sie sind alle sampt nit gnůg mit iren

Ja das ich euch recht vnderweiſe. ſzo merckt auff / du
ſalt vor allenn dingen (widder ſanct Peters gebewde
noch ablas angeſehen) deynẽ nehſten armẽ geben / wil
tu etwas geben. Wan eſz aber dahyn kumpt / das nye-
mandt yn deyner ſtat mehr iſt der hulff bedarff (das
ob gott wil nymer geſcheen ſall) dañ ſaltu geben ſzo du
wilt tzu den kirchen / altarn / ſchmuck / kelich / die in dey
ner ſtadt ſeyn. Und wen das auch nu nit mehr not iſt /
Dañ aller erſt / ſzo du wilt / magſtu geben zu dẽ gebew
de. S. Peters adder anderwo. Auch ſoltu dennoch nit
das vmb ablas willen thun. dañ ſant Paul ſpricht
Wer ſeynẽ hauſz genoſzẽ nit wol thut / iſt keyn Chriſtẽ
vnd erger dañ ein heyde / vñ halts dafur frey / wer dir
ãders ſagt / der vorfurt dich / adder ſucht yhe dein ſeel
in deynem Beutell vnd fund er pfenning darinne / das
were ym lieber dañ all ſeelẽ. Szo ſprichſtu. Szo werd
ich nymer mehr ablas loſzen. Antwort ich / das hab
ich ſchon obẽ geſagt / Das meyn will / begirde / bitt vñ
ratt iſt / das nyemandt ablas loſze / laſz die faulen vnd
ſchlefferigen Chriſten / ablas loſzen / gang du fur dich.

Czum Sibenczehenden. Der ablas iſt nich geboten
auch nicht geratẽ / ſunderñ von der dinger czall / die czu
gelaſſen vñ erleubt werdẽ. darumb iſt es nit eyn werck
des gehorſams / auch nit vordinſtlich / ſunderñ eyn auſz
czug des gehorſams. Darumb wiewol man / nyemant
weren ſoll / den czu loſzen / ſzo ſolt mã doch alle Chriſtẽ
daruon czihen / and zu den wercken vñ peynen / die do
nachgelaſſen / reyczen vnd ſterckenñ.

Czum Achtczehendẽ. Ab die ſeelen auſz dẽ fegfewr
geczogen werden durch den ablas / weyſz ich nit / vñge
leub das auch noch nich / wiewol das eczlich new doc
tores ſagen / aber iſt yhn vnmuglich czubeweren / auch
hat es die kirch noch nit beſchloſſen / darumb czu meh-

opinien/das ſie ein predig befeſtigen ſolten.

¶ Zů dem zwentzigoſten. Ob etzlich mich nun wol einen kätzer ſchelten/den ſoliche warheit ſeer ſchedlich iſt jm̄ ka ſtē. So acht ich doch ſolich jr geplärr nit groſz/ dañ etzlich finſter gebürne die/die Bibel nie gerochen/die Chriſtenliche lere nie geläſen/jr eygen leren nie vorſtandē/ſunder jn yren gelöcherten vnd zerriſznen opiniē vyl nah vorweſen. Dañ hetten ſie die verſtanden/ſo wüſtē ſie/das ſie niemādt ſolten leſtern/vnuerhort vnd vnuberwundē; doch got geb yn vnd vnſz rechten ſynn. Amen.

Getruckt nach Chriſt geburt Tauſent fünffhundert vnd ym achtzehēdē Jar.

rer sicherheyt/ vil besser ist es/ das du vor sie selbst bittest vñ wirckest/ dan disz ist bewerter vñ ist gewisz

¶ Czum Neunczehendē. In dissen puncten hab ich nit czweyffel/ vnnd sind gnugsam in der schrifft gegrund. Darumb sol ir auch keyn czweyffel haben/ vñ last doctores Scholasticos/ scholasticos sein/ sie sein alsampt nit gnug/ mit yhren opinien/ das sie eyne prediget befestigenn soltenn.

¶ Czum czwenczigsten. Ab etzlich mich nu wol eynen keczer schelten/ den solch warheyt seer schedlich ist im kasten. Szo acht ich doch solch geplerre nit grosz/ suntemal das nit thun/ dañ eczlich finster ghyrne/ die die Biblien nie gerochē/ die Christenlichē lerer nie geleszē yhr eigen lerer nie vorstanden/ sundern in yhren lochereten vnd czurissen opinien vill nah vorwesen/ dā hetthen sie die vorstanden szo wisten sie/ das sie nyemādt solten lestern/ vnuorhort vñ vnuberwundē/ doch got geb yhn/ vnd vns rechten sinn. Amen.

¶ Getruckt Nach Christ geburt Tausent funff hundert vñ ym achczehenden Jar.

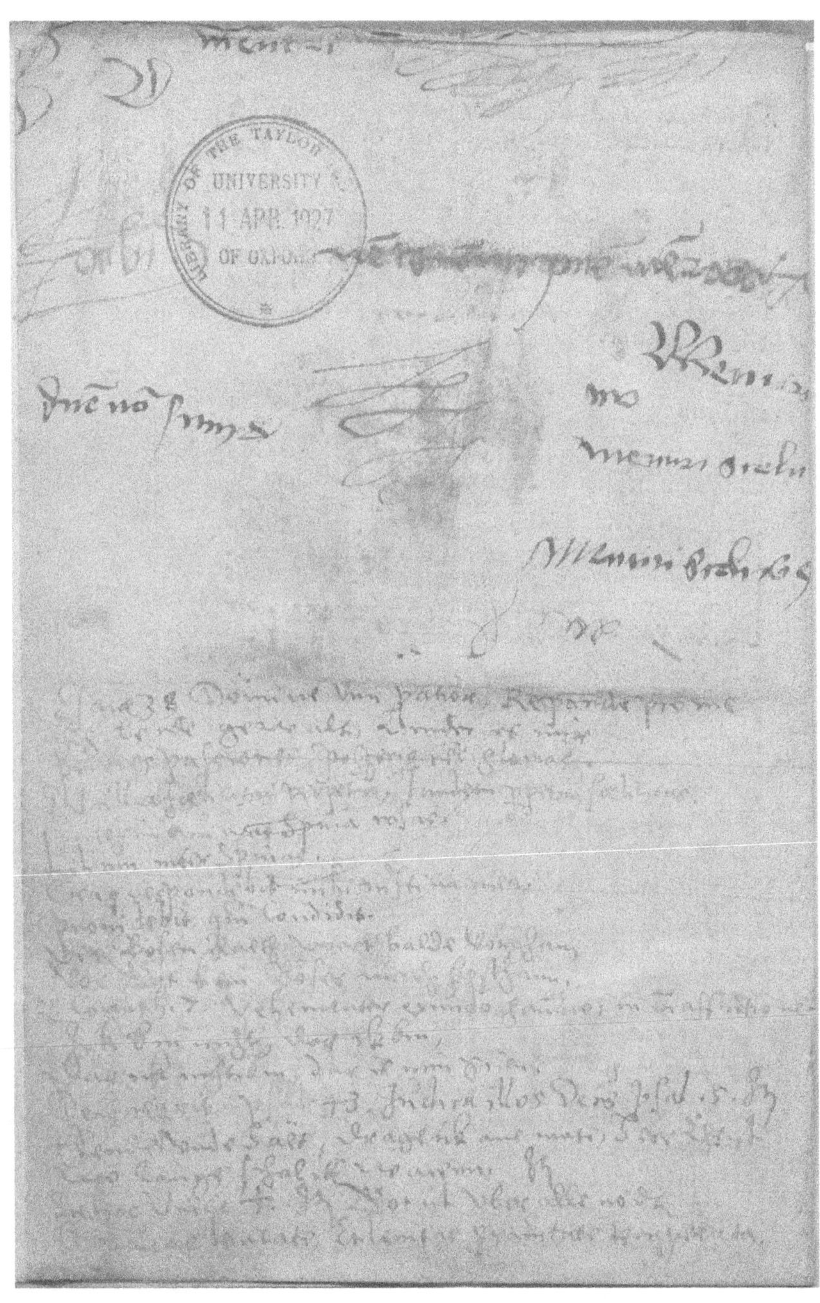

www.ingramcontent.com/pod-product-compliance
Lightning Source LLC
Chambersburg PA
CBHW071002120726
47910CB00004B/1347

* 9 7 8 0 9 9 5 4 5 6 4 2 6 *